D1544562

THE SCOTTISH DEBATE

THE SCOTTISH DEBATE

Essays on Scottish Nationalism

EDITED BY

NEIL MacCORMICK

London

OXFORD UNIVERSITY PRESS

GLASGOW NEW YORK

1970

*Oxford University Press, Ely House, London, W.*1

GLASGOW NEW YORK TORONTO MELBOURNE WELLINGTON
CAPE TOWN SALISBURY IBADAN NAIROBI DAR ES SALAAM LUSAKA ADDIS ABABA
BOMBAY CALCUTTA MADRAS KARACHI LAHORE DACCA
KUALA LUMPUR SINGAPORE HONG KONG TOKYO

SBN 19 215174 6

320.54
S431

Printed in Great Britain by
Neill & Co. Ltd., Edinburgh

CONTENTS

INTRODUCTION

This book is founded on the supposition that the present demand for greater political independence in Scotland is not merely a nine days' wonder but will remain a live issue in British politics in the foreseeable future. The objectives at which the book is aimed are to contribute to a clearer understanding of the nature of the Scottish national movement in historical and comparative terms, and to facilitate rational judgment of the issues at stake by presenting a debate on the arguments for and against home rule in one form or another.

Although the book is concerned primarily with Scottish nationalism alone, it should be of interest to all citizens of the United Kingdom since the question is whether the Kingdom should remain united. That is a question of more than Scottish interest. Indeed, I may perhaps be permitted to remark that as a Scotsman presently living and working in England I find around me among my English friends and colleagues a remarkable and even alarming unawareness of the matters with which the book deals; yet these matters are of real importance for all of us in Britain. So I hope the book will find some English readers; and even more I hope that, if it does, they will find it illuminating.

The contributors are a varied group of politicians and academics, varied both in their interests and in their political views. Thus the book as a whole consists of a debate, not of the advocacy of any particular point of view. Since the essays approach the central question of Scottish independence from widely differing points of view there is not, I hope, too much repetition from one to another, although there is inevitably a certain degree of overlapping between some of the essays.

This debate is a vital one for us all, yet it has provoked very little serious writing in the course of a history to whose respectable length Professor Young's essay testifies. Recently, there have been a number of valuable studies of the problem, and it is to be hoped that there will be more yet. Whatever is to happen to Scotland and Britain, it should surely happen only after serious and rational argument. No doubt politics is in the end founded in large part upon prejudice and emotion, but these ought to be tempered and

1

tested in the fire of critical discussion. In so far as all the present essayists have one object, it is to contribute to that process.

It would be impossible in one volume to take account of all possible points of view, or to deal with every relevant area of argument; I am myself particularly conscious that no room is here given specifically to literary or more general cultural matters, for which the only excuse is that this has been one of the less neglected fields. The best one can hope to do in producing a symposium of this kind is to make room for a reasonable variety of opinions and special interests; I shall be well pleased if the balance of the book seems fair.

I ought perhaps briefly to mention my own political position, so that any editorial bias may at least be open. I am myself convinced by the arguments in favour of creating some sort of parliament and government in Scotland, but I remain unsure as to what sort would, on the whole, be best, for reasons which are sufficiently stated in my own essay. Despite being unconvinced that independence would be the best course for Scotland or for the rest of Britain, I am a member of the Scottish National Party, since it seems to me abundantly clear that neither of the two large parties is likely to take the smallest step towards any worthwhile form of self-government for Scotland (or for Wales, for that matter, to say nothing of the regions of England) unless they are subjected to powerful electoral pressures of a quite unequivocal kind. The Liberal Party, whose policies are at least as attractive to me, seems likely to remain a minority party; and Liberal successes are not unequivocal pointers to a demand for home rule, as those of the National Party are.

In practical terms, as I state in my essay, it seems perfectly obvious that devolution would have to precede independence, so that if devolution worked well we could abandon the notion of proceeding to independence. Therefore, I see nothing foolish or irrational in supporting the National Party while remaining unconvinced of the value of its long-term objectives. It seems to me rather like voting Labour without swallowing 'Clause Four' whole.

It is, however, a matter for regret that the polarization which party politics produces tends to create artificial conflicts. This book perhaps illustrates to what extent there is general agreement on the proposition that some greater degree of local control of

Scottish affairs is desirable, however deep-seated the differences may be on the form which that should take. The context of party politics magnifies differences of opinion and obscures the middle ground. But previous attempts to capture the middle ground by such all-party groups as the Home Rule Association and the Covenant Association have failed because they could not pose a serious electoral threat to the large parties. *Faute de mieux* one can only hope that a workable consensus may emerge out of the conflict, and that the extremes of debate will never lead to extreme and ill-considered action.

The essays were delivered to the Press on 30 June 1969, so that none of the authors has had the opportunity to take account of any later developments, such as the publication of the Report of the Royal Commission on Local Government in Scotland (the Wheatley Report), or of the 'Scottish Budget' issued by the Treasury (see p. 123.).

I owe a great deal to the good will both of my contributors—particularly Douglas Young and Donald Dewar, who helped to get the book off the ground at the very beginning—and of the publishers, who bore my editorial inexperience with admirable equanimity. I obtained great help and encouragement from my wife, and helpful criticism of my own essay from my colleague Alan Rodger, to both of whom I am grateful; and I am indebted to Miss Patricia Lloyd for her secretarial help. If this had been my own book and not a symposium I should have dedicated it to my parents, from whose labours on behalf of a humane and liberal Scottish Nationalism I have inherited my prejudice in favour of home rule.

Neil MacCormick

ABBREVIATIONS

The following abbreviations are used in the text:

C.B.I.	Confederation of British Industries
D.E.A.	Department of Economic Affairs
E.E.C.	European Economic Community
G.L.C.	Greater London Council
N.A.T.O.	North Atlantic Treaty Organisation
R.E.P.	Regional Employment Premium
S.E.T.	Selective Employment Tax
S.N.P.	Scottish National Party

1

A Sketch History of
Scottish Nationalism

DOUGLAS YOUNG

The campaign for self-government by the nation in the northern part of the island of Britain has been continuous, in one form or other, since A.D. 80, when the Roman attempt at conquest by Cn. Julius Agricola, father-in-law of the historian Tacitus, met with a concerted resistance by a federation of the *civitates* of the Britons in Caledonia, north of the Forth-Clyde isthmus. These Celts, speaking a language nearer to Welsh than to Gaelic, were nicknamed *Picti* by the Romans, meaning 'Tattooees', in reference to their adherence to the old magical or heraldic tattoo designs of the British Celts. The Celtic word for design, *cruth*, gave rise to the Gaelic ethnic name *Cruithni*, used of the Picts, and to the Greek and Roman ethnics, *Pretanoi*, *Britanni*, *Britones*, which derived from the P-Celtic labialization of the Gaelic ethnic, and gave rise to the modern terms *Briton* and *Britain*.

The organic continuity of the Celtic nation that withstood Roman imperialist attacks, from A.D. 80 intermittently to 399, can be traced through the Dark Ages, under a variety of ethnic names, of which the most authentic and persistent is Welsh and Gaelic *Alban*, Greek *Albion*. Regional cantons, under local kings and their client aristocracies, were more or less confederated under a High Kingship of Alban, to which succession could be made through females, as with the modern British monarchy. Thus, in the ninth century, the High Kingship of Alban devolved on a line of Irish sub-kings holding lands in Ulster and Argyll, using the Gaelic language, and having the support of the powerful group of monasteries founded by St. Columba, an Irish Gael. Accordingly, from towards 1100, the learned name 'Scotti' began to supersede older ethnics in monkish Latin documents, and to cease to be

5

applied to the Irish or *Hiberni*. Thus the kingdom came to be normally called Scotland, and its inhabitants were termed Scots, instead of Britons, Picts, or Albanians. Popular tradition grasped the central truth that the nation had never been conquered, whether by Romans, Scandinavians, or the Germanic tribes settled in England.

The Scottish national legislature is first styled by a contemporary a *parlement* in the year 1173, and a Scottish Parliament, variously constituted, continued to legislate till 1707. There are today still in force some 276 Acts of the pre-1707 Scottish Parliament, concerning which a leading nineteenth-century historian, Sir Archibald Alison, wrote thus:

> In truth, the early precocity of Scotland in legislative wisdom, and the extraordinary provisions made by its native Parliament in remote periods, not only for the well-being of the people but the coercion alike of regal tyranny and aristocratic oppression, and the instruction, relief and security of the poorer classes, is one of the most remarkable facts in the whole history of modern Europe.

Attempts at incorporating union of the Scottish and English Parliaments were made by the first Plantagenet Edward in 1304, by James VI and I from 1603, and Oliver Cromwell from 1651; but they all broke down from Scottish and, hardly less, from English hostility to their provisions. The first major loss of sovereignty by Scotland arose from the accidental consequences of a sixteenth-century royal marriage, and the departure of the Stewart dynasty to England after James VI inherited in 1603 the thrones of England, Ireland, and—in theory still—France. This led to the emergence of Great Britain, so called to distinguish it from the Duchy of Britanny in France, as a dynastic multi-national state, somewhat like the Austro-Hungarian multi-national union under the Hapsburgs, which collapsed in 1918.

The union of the crowns in 1603 did not necessitate a union of parliaments, and for a time, from 1640, the Scottish constitution was substantially that now enjoyed by such dominions of the British Crown as Canada and New Zealand. But in 1707 the Scots and English Parliaments ratified a legislative amalgamation by international treaty, constituting the Parliament of the United Kingdom of Great Britain. This Treaty kept separate the Established Church of Scotland, with its presbyterian government, and the Scots law and lawcourts. The motives of its promoters were mixed; but it seems to have been primarily an anti-papalist coalition, aiming to secure the succession of a Protestant monarch. As an inducement to some Scots, in the mercantilist era, the Treaty provided for an insular common market, extended to the overseas dependencies.

Political and religious interests were dominant, and any economic advantages envisaged in the union of 1707 were slow to accrue. In 1713 a Scots motion to repeal it was lost in the House of Lords by only four votes. The Jacobite party exploited Scots patriotic resentments in favour of the Jacobite risings of 1715 and 1745; but by 1745 the bulk of the Scottish public was wholly indifferent to any scheme to restore a papalist claimant backed by French arms. Meanwhile, as the eighteenth century developed, Scotland saw a notable increase of wealth from the agricultural revolution, largely derived from Dutch models known to Scotsmen pursuing legal and medical studies at Leiden and Utrecht. Some fresh capital accrued also from fortunes made by Scots in the old English colonies overseas, and Scots soldiers played a major part in the new British conquests of Canada and India after 1750. The first breakthrough of Scots careerists in politics was with the premiership of Lord Bute in the 1760s. Scottish nationalist feelings were frequently manifested in all strata of society, as appears from the correspondence, for example, of David Hume and of James Boswell; but serious political agitation to alter the union of 1707 did not start till after the American and French revolutions.

The first democratically organized nationalist movement after 1707 was the Society of the Friends of the People, led by Thomas Muir, who in 1793 was transported to Australia for sedition. This body demanded manhood suffrage, and separate parliaments for Scotland and Ireland. Among its subscribers was the poet Robert Burns, who wrote his national anthem, 'Scots wha hae', in connection with the trial of Muir. It was banned as seditious by the reactionary Tory governments in the period after Waterloo.

In the early industrial struggles of the wage-earners in central Scotland the demand for a Scottish parliament was a frequent theme. For example, in 1820, the Radical leader 'Pearlie' Wilson, of Strathaven, and his fellow weavers carried a banner with the slogan *Scotland Free or a Desert*, when they marched out, misled by *agents provocateurs*, to confront the Tory dragoons at the

'Battle of Bonnymuir'. Wilson and others were executed for their part in the agitation.

During the 1840s the Chartists made a Scottish parliament one of their demands. From 1853 it seems possible to trace an unbroken nexus of personnel and organizations in the expression of the demand for self-government, with inevitable shifts of emphasis. In 1853 a National Association for the Vindication of Scottish Rights was formed, led by Lord Provost Duncan McLaren of Edinburgh, a leading Liberal; Professor W. E. Aytoun, a Tory and poet; and the Radical journalist Patrick Dove. Its main immediate demand was the restoration of the Secretaryship of State for Scotland, which had lapsed since 1746, when the handling of the Rising was entrusted to the Lord Advocate as chief Scottish Minister. So slow and fumbling has been the handling of Scottish affairs that the demand for a Secretaryship of State for Scotland, made in 1853, was not fully met till 1926, a lapse of 73 years.

In 1869 a majority of Scots M.P.s asked Prime Minister Gladstone to appoint a Secretary for Scotland. A Commission was appointed, and recommended the appointment of a parliamentary Under-Secretary at the Home Office, but neither Gladstone nor Disraeli took action. In 1877 Sir Graham Campbell, M.P. for Kirkcaldy Burghs, demanded a Scottish Grand Committee, to consist mainly of the Scots M.P.s, as an interim step towards ultimate self-government for Scotland within a federal system. In 1880 the young fifth Earl of Rosebery was Gladstone's host during the famous Midlothian campaign, and began to have influence with the Grand Old Man of Liberalism. In 1881 Rosebery, with the Duke of Argyll and others, proposed in the Lords a Secretaryship, and Gladstone created an Under-Secretaryship at the Home Office, with Rosebery as first incumbent. After two years Rosebery resigned the position in disgust at the London bureaucrats' lack of cooperation. In January 1884 the Convention of Royal Burghs organized an important all-party rally in Edinburgh, at which leading Scots Tories backed the mainly Liberal demand for a Secretaryship for Scotland. They included the Marquis of Lothian, Arthur Balfour, and Lord Balfour of Burleigh. This all-party coalition secured quick results, for a Liberal Bill of 1884 was put through in August 1885 by the Tory Prime Minister Lord Salisbury. The first

Secretary for Scotland was the Tory Duke of Richmond and Gordon.

The 1880s perhaps mark the highest point so far of Scottish nationalist agitation concerted on an all-party basis and securing practical legislative results. The decade also saw a considerable cultural revival, of which Robert Louis Stevenson's poems in Scots, or Lallans, as he called it, were one memorable manifestation. In 1886 an all-party Scottish Home Rule Association was founded, led mainly by Liberals, who held the majority of Scots seats at almost every election from 1832 to 1914, but with the backing of leading Conservatives, and early Socialists, such as Keir Hardie and Ramsay Macdonald.

When Keir Hardie stood for parliament at Mid Lanark in 1888 his election address stated: 'I am strongly in favour of Home Rule for Scotland, being convinced that until we have a Parliament of our own we cannot obtain the many and great reforms on which I believe the people of Scotland have set their hearts.' Keir Hardie went on to found, in August 1888, the Scottish Labour Party, the first political party in the United Kingdom to try for independent parliamentary representation of wage-earners. Its first president was the remarkable traveller and writer, R. B. Cunninghame Graham, then a Radical M.P. Keir Hardie, as secretary, went as the Scottish Labour Party delegate to the foundation conference of the Second International in 1889. In 1893, having been elected M.P. for a constituency in England, Hardie helped to form the Independent Labour Party (I.L.P.) on a United Kingdom basis, and in 1894 the Scottish Labour Party became a Scottish Council of the I.L.P., the larger body having adopted the Scottish Home Rule principle.

A motion for Scottish Home Rule was moved in the House of Commons in 1889 by the vice-president of the Scottish Labour Party, Dr. G. B. Clark, whose candidature in Caithness had been sponsored by the Highland Land League, political organ of the crofters claiming security of land-tenure. Scots M.P.s voted against it by 22 to 19, the U.K. majority against being 200 to 79. But on bringing the motion forward again in 1890, Dr. Clark got a Scots majority of 26 to 15 in favour, the U.K. majority being still against it, by 181 to 141.

The first 'Home Rule All Round' motion was introduced by Dr. Clark in 1891, envisaging four sub-parliaments, for Scotland,

England, Ireland, and Wales, with limited powers devolved from
the Imperial Parliament. The House was counted out. Next year,
1892, W. A. Hunter introduced a novel proposal that the Scots
M.P.s in the U.K. Parliament should hold an autumn legislative
session in Scotland, and that their legislation should be given the
royal assent automatically. The House was counted out. Later
in 1892 Clark again moved for Home Rule All Round, winning a
Scots majority (24–14), but finding the U.K. majority against
(74–54). A similar result was seen in 1893, but in 1894 a U.K.
majority of 180 to 170 carried Sir Henry Dalziel's motion for
Home Rule All Round. The Scots majority was 38 to 20, and the
Englishman then serving as Secretary for Scotland, Sir George
Trevelyan, helped to effect the U.K. majority. But in 1895 a
renewed motion by Dalziel, with a Scots majority of 30 to 14, was
turned down by a U.K. majority of 128 to 102. In the later 1890s
there was a jingo imperialist phase, and in 1899 D. V. Pirie's
attempt to move a Scottish Home Rule Bill failed to pass its first
reading.

The Secretaryship for Scotland initiated in 1885 had grown
mainly out of the Home Office functions in Scotland, with the
addition of some areas of government taken over from the
Treasury, the Privy Council, and the Local Government Board
for England. This administrative devolution was partly paralleled
in 1894–5 by the institution of a Scottish Grand Committee,
consisting of the Scots M.P.s with fifteen others added to ensure
a fair reflection of the balance of parties in the whole House. The
Tory governments of 1895 to 1905 let it lapse, but the Liberals
under Sir Henry Campbell-Bannerman revived it in 1907
permanently, to deal with the committee stage of Bills pronounced
non-controversial.

In 1897 was formed the Scottish Trades Union Congress, of
delegates from unions operating in Scotland and from Trades
Councils in the cities. This S.T.U.C. formed, in 1900, a Scottish
Workers' Parliamentary Election Committee some weeks before
Keir Hardie and others set up in London the Labour Representa-
tion Committee that grew into the Labour Party. At the 1906
general election the Scottish T.U.C.'s body campaigned as the
Scottish Labour Party. Home Rule was taken for granted as a
desideratum in these agencies. During the Boer War a Young
Scots Society was formed, to protect public meetings from

jingoistic roughnecks and to promote progressive causes, including Home Rule. Their influence countered that of imperialists within the Liberal Party, and helped the return of a Radical government under Campbell-Bannerman in 1906. In this atmosphere D. V. Pirie moved in 1908 a Government of Scotland Bill, proposing federal devolution, and secured majorities on the first reading, Scots 41–9, U.K. 257–102. In 1911 Sir Henry Dalziel moved a similar Bill, with a Scots majority on the first reading 31–4, the U.K. majority 172–73. Home Rule All Round was revived in 1912 in a motion by Dr. Chapple, with a Scots majority 43–6, U.K. 226–128. MacCallum Scott's Government of the United Kingdom Bill in 1912 secured a U.K. majority on its first reading of 264–212, Scots 43–7.

The highwater mark of Liberal Home Rule agitation was seen in 1913, when Sir W. H. Cowan's Scottish Home Rule Bill passed not only on the first but on the crucial second reading, by 204 to 159, the Scots favouring it by 45 to 8. A. J. Balfour, for the Unionists, as Scots Conservatives were called from 1912, counter-proposed a scheme for all four nations of the U.K., on the basis of what he termed 'a glorified county council'. In May 1913 the Liberal Prime Minister, H. H. Asquith, announced that his government would put through an act for Scottish Home Rule in the current session of Parliament. But contentious elements in Ulster were at that time opposing any parallel scheme for Ireland, and the Tory House of Lords would probably not have agreed to Asquith's plan for Scotland. At any rate it was shelved, and with the outbreak of war in 1914 most Scots nationalist activists betook themselves to securing independence for Serbia and Belgium, many of them being killed.

The Scottish Home Rule Association resumed in 1917 its political work, interrupted by the war, now under the leadership of Keir Hardie's friend Roland E. Muirhead, as secretary, and Thomas Johnston, founder-editor of the independent Socialist weekly *Forward*, started in Glasgow in 1906, and described by Bernard Shaw as 'the first paper worth a workman's tuppence'. While the membership of the S.H.R.A. continued to be all-party, Labour and I.L.P. elements were strong. The Labour Party was constituted with an individual membership in 1918, and its conference of June 1918 adopted a resolution, No. 13, on constitutional devolution, asserting, in part:

some early devolution from Westminster of both legislation and administration is imperatively called for . . . along with the grant of Home Rule to Ireland there should be constituted separate statutory legislative assemblies for Scotland, Wales, and even England, with autonomous administration in matters of local concern.

This 1918 conference resolution, mainly drafted by Sidney Webb, also advocated retention of a Parliament at Westminster to be 'a federal assembly for the United Kingdom', and envisaged a 'Cabinet for Commonwealth affairs for the Britannic Commonwealth as a whole', bringing in ministers representing the Dominions and India to sit with ministers responsible for the Federal Departments of the United Kingdom.

How these principles were disseminated to the masses is seen from leaflet No. 19 (New Series) issued by the Labour Party in the 1918 general election, which ran thus:

What the Labour Party means by HOME RULE ALL ROUND and a Democratic Administration for the Whole British Commonwealth of Nations. Labour Believes in Self-Government. The Labour Party is pledged to a scheme of separate statutory Legislatures for Scotland, Wales, and even England, as well as for Ireland, as part of the larger plan of constitutional reform which will transform the British Empire into a Britannic Federation, or COMMONWEALTH OF BRITISH SELF-GOVERNING COMMUNITIES. The Labour Party advocates the establishment of these local parliaments to deal with both legislation and administration in matters of exclusively local concern, on the basis of complete autonomy, with A COUNCIL FOR THE WHOLE BRITISH COMMON-WEALTH. The Labour Party, having experience of the congestion of the Parliamentary machine, urges the necessity of having a Council, without coercive authority, to deal with inter-dominion and international affairs and suggest the necessary legislation to the several parliaments. This Council should exercise control over the Ministers responsible for the departments of the Federal Government, who will form, with the Ministers representing the overseas Dominions and India, A CABINET FOR THE COMMONWEALTH AS A WHOLE.

The Labour Party believes that separate legislatures on the federal plan would strengthen nationalist sentiment, which means more than the intensive cultivation of race pride and the preservation of national customs, traditions, and culture; they would lead every such self-governing community to take a deeper interest in the work of the LOCAL PARLIAMENTS.

The Labour Party recognizes that responsibility for the maintenance of the British Empire, comprising many races, many religions, many languages, many communities in every stage of political and economic development, some still in a state of political tutelage, rests upon THE PARLIAMENT AT WESTMINSTER. It must therefore be relieved of purely local affairs which now burden the parliamentary machine and exhaust the energies of Ministers, and devote itself to its duties as the Federal Assembly for the United Kingdom and to building up this vast Commonwealth of Peoples. Vote for the Labour Candidate and HOME RULE ALL ROUND!

In pursuance of these officially endorsed Labour principles, Labour, I.L.P. and Cooperative candidates in Scotland supported the Scottish Home Rule Association, to which were affiliated many Trade Union branches, Cooperative Societies, and local authorities, especially burghs. A peak year for this Labour and Socialist stream of nationalist propaganda seems to have been 1923, when, at the annual commemoration of Sir William Wallace at Elderslie, William Adamson, later Secretary of State for Scotland, supported the demand for a Scottish Parliament, and on the same day in George Square, Glasgow, there were six platforms, containing eighteen Labour M.P.s, enthusiastically haranguing enthusiastic large crowds on the topic. Reflecting this widespread zeal, a Glasgow Labour M.P., George Buchanan, moved in May 1924, during the first minority Labour government of Ramsay Macdonald, a Government of Scotland Bill, on the lines of the pre-1914 Liberal Home Rule Bills. Buchanan was promised the support of 56 of the then Scots M.P.s (all 32 Labour and allied M.P.s, 23 Liberals, and one Scots Tory, Major Donaldson, of Dumfries Burghs). Ramsay Macdonald promised it parliamentary time, but his government fell before more was done.

Buchanan's Bill proposed 'an extension of the policy of devolution within the United Kingdom'. It provided for a single-chamber Parliament of 148 members to deal with Scottish affairs, and the continuance of Scottish representation in the Commons of the U.K. 'until separate provision is made for devolution in England and Wales'. In effect, it would have set up a Scottish sub-parliament with roughly the powers of the Parliament of Northern Ireland, with a joint Exchequer Board.

The failure of the first Macdonald government to secure
re-election gave an impetus to Scottish Socialists to press their
demand for Scottish self-government, the view being taken that
Scotland was a favourable sector for Socialist advance, and that
Socialist planning was needed to secure the Scottish people from
the effects of the post-war dislocation of traditional markets and
from the growing insular capitalist rationalization, whereby
Scottish industries were being taken over, and sometimes closed
down, by English competitors. In 1926 a Scottish National
Convention was held, sponsored by the Scottish Home Rule
Association, whose president was Robert Smillie, leader of the
Scottish coalminers. It was backed by Tom Johnston, the elder
John Wheatley, James Maxton, and a majority of Socialist M.P.s,
about half the Scots Liberals (others having been frightened that
Home Rule could lead to domination by the supposed Socialist
extremists of the 'Red Clydeside'), some Tories, and many trade
unions, cooperative societies, and local authorities—largely
influenced by Sir Henry Keith, leading man in the Convention
of Royal Burghs.

This National Convention endorsed the principle of Dominion
Status for Scotland, consistent with the impending Statute of
Westminster whereby the British Empire was being converted
into a Commonwealth of self-governing states linked by the
Crown. A Government of Scotland Bill was moved by the Rev.
James Barr, seconded by Tom Johnston, and had its second
reading on 13 May 1927, when it was talked out by Tories. The
Barr-Johnston Bill provided for a single-chamber parliament for
Scotland, of 148 Members, having the powers of a separate
dominion under the Crown, which was to be represented in
Scotland 'by a Lord High Commissioner who shall be appointed
in like manner as the Governor-General of Canada' (in the words
of the prefatory Memorandum). Any question of interpretation
'shall be decided according to the principle that Scotland is a
sovereign state whose sovereignty is exercised on the authority of
the Scottish Parliament' (par. 31). Scots representation was to
cease at Westminster, but a Joint Council of the Scottish and
'Imperial' Parliaments was to consult on 'Joint Services', namely
the Navy, Army, Air Force, and Foreign Office, and the sharing
of their costs. It was provided (par. 20) that, in default of agreement, 'it shall be within the option of either Government to

demand that these be separate services for each country.' In the apportionment of the public debt (par. 11), in default of agreement, it was proposed to seek arbitration by 'one or more independent persons being citizens of the British Community of Free Nations, who shall be empowered to gather all the evidence necessary to enable them to reach a decision.'

Barr's Bill of 1927 was a more daring and intransigent approach to the inter-national relations of Scotland and the other nations in the unhappily United Kingdom than Buchanan's Bill of 1924. The Labour Conference of 1929 re-affirmed the 1918 Sidney Webb formulation of principles on federal self-government for Scotland and the other nations in the British Commonwealth, and that is still theoretically the Labour Party's latest delegate conference formulation of principle.

The Tory rejection in 1927 of Barr's Bill and the demands of the 1926 Scottish National Convention led to the formation in 1928 of the National Party of Scotland out of four groups. These were the Scots National League, largely activated by Thomas H. Gibson, with its monthly publication, *The Scots Independent*; the Scottish National Movement, led by the poet and anthropologist Lewis Spence; the Glasgow University Scottish Nationalist Association, led by a young lawyer of I.L.P. background, John M. MacCormick; and a section of the Home Rule Association, led by its long-time secretary, R. E. Muirhead. The National Party of Scotland aimed, in effect, at Dominion Status on the lines of the Barr-Johnston Bill sponsored by the Labour M.P.s; but its basis of association specifically excluded members of other parties, including Barr and Johnston. It rushed into a by-election early in 1929, in North Midlothian, and secured less than 10 per cent of the votes, thus giving a false impression of the public support for the demand made by the Labour promoters of Barr's Bill.

In 1932 a Scottish Party was formed, of less intransigent and more rightist elements, including Professor Andrew Dewar Gibb, a former Tory candidate; Sir Alexander MacEwen, a leading Liberal; James Duke of Montrose, and many smaller businessmen and academics and people prominent in local government. It did not contest elections, but worked as a pressure group. After the sweeping success of the three-party 'National' Government coalition at the 1931 British general election, some Scots nationalists envisaged the possibility of forming a Scottish national coalition; and negotiations led to the fusion of the National Party of Scotland with the Scottish Party, in 1934, under the title Scottish National Party, its basis of association allowing office-bearers, candidates, and members to be also members of the main U.K. parties. The bulk of the S.N.P. members were disgruntled Socialists or Liberals, with a few Tories, and many persons new to politics. Labour and other M.P.s occasionally supported its platform, and it made some impact at by-elections. William Power got 37 per cent of the poll in Argyll, Dewar Gibb 39 per cent in the Scottish Universities.

After 1935 the S.N.P., with John MacCormick as secretary, participated to some extent in the 'Popular Front' against Fascism led by Sir Stafford Cripps, and sought to organize a National Convention in 1939 on the lines of the Home Rule Association's Convention of 1926 that had drafted Barr's Bill. The 1939 war caused the Convention to be postponed. Before the war, in 1937, the annual conference of the S.N.P. had voted that members of military age should refuse to be conscripted by any non-Scottish government, and in the event some young men did refuse. Among them was a Lecturer in Greek at Aberdeen University, named Douglas Young, who was in April 1942 sentenced to twelve months' imprisonment for resistance to the so-called National Service Act as contrary to the Treaty of Union. While liberated on bail pending appeal, he was elected Chairman by the S.N.P. annual conference of May 1942. Shortly thereafter John MacCormick and some other prominent members withdrew, and formed a non-party pressure group, eventually called Scottish Convention. With Dr. Robert McIntyre as secretary, the S.N.P. revived remarkably, and got rid of its long-standing indebtedness. At a three-cornered by-election in 1944 Douglas Young came near election with 42 per cent of the poll, at Kirkcaldy Burghs, and in a straight fight in April 1945 Dr. Robert McIntyre was elected M.P. for Motherwell, with 52 per cent. But when the wartime political truce ended, at the general election of July 1945, the S.N.P.'s eight candidates did poorly, only two saving their deposits.

In 1936 Tom Johnston had taken the lead in organizing a working party, The London Scots Self-Government Committee, which had the support of many Scots and some Welsh M.P.s, and of Clement Attlee, who, as Leader of the Labour Party, re-affirmed to the London Committee, in February 1938, that the Labour Party 'stood by their policy announced in 1929 which had never been altered. It was that they favoured a separate legislature for Scotland with autonomous powers in matters of local concern'. In a Preface to the Committee's publication, *Plan for Scotland*, by Thomas Burns, Attlee wrote:

> There was at one time a tendency among Socialists to underrate the force of National Sentiment. Today we ought all to recognize that nationalism has an immense attractive force for good or evil. Suppressed, it may poison the political life of a nation. Given its proper place it can enrich it. . . . In this pamphlet, self-government is put in its right place as part of a plan for giving a better and fuller life to all the people of these islands. There is plenty of spadework to be done in working out the best means of effecting the most fruitful co-operation between the three nations inhabiting Britain. It is work worth doing, because it is of importance not only for our own people but for an example to other nations whose destinies are linked together, but who have not yet reached the degree of co-operation attained here. Above all, I commend the careful consideration of the economic questions which many so-called nationalists ignore.

At the general election of 1945 the Labour Party's manifesto said nothing about Home Rule, but its Scottish office issued a manifesto listing 'A Scottish Parliament for Scottish Affairs' as second priority after the defeat of Japan; and 24 out of the 37 Labour M.P.s returned from Scotland personally undertook to promote such a Scottish Parliament. To focus the public interest, John MacCormick's Scottish Convention organization convened in March 1947 a Scottish National Assembly, widely representative of local authorities, trade union branches, presbyteries, and other bodies, with a sprinkling of M.P.s and peers of all parties. It voted for the establishment of a Scottish sub-parliament, as an interim step, much on the lines of the Labour Party Scottish Council's 1941 *Plan for Post-War Scotland*, in which the Scots Members of the U.K. Parliament were to function as a 'Scottish Parliament for Scottish Affairs'.

The Labour Government's reply to this demand was a White Paper in January 1948, brought in by Arthur Woodburn, as Secretary of State, which slightly extended the powers of the Scottish Grand Committee to debate non-controversial Scottish

Bills and to discuss estimates for the departments under the Secretary of State for Scotland. In October 1949 the Scottish National Assembly launched the 'Scottish Covenant' pledging its signatories 'in all loyalty to the Crown, and within the framework of the United Kingdom, to do everything in our power to secure for Scotland a Parliament with adequate legislative authority in Scottish affairs'. The detailed proposals of the National Covenant Committee were on the lines of Buchanan's Bill of 1924, for a sub-parliament with slightly greater powers than Northern Ireland; and this proposition received support from some two million Scots out of an electorate of about 3,600,000. Mr. Attlee took note of the Covenant, and dismissed Arthur Woodburn in favour of Hector McNeil, who, as Labour candidate at Greenock in 1945, had stated:

> If my Tory opponent (Lord Malcolm Douglas-Hamilton) is unwilling to pledge himself to a measure of self-government for Scotland, he should take off the kilt he wears, and not attempt to mislead people into thinking he is a patriotic Scot. The Scottish Labour M.P.s have backed up every Home Rule Bill presented to Parliament this century.

Attlee in 1950 took the line that, before legislation could be considered, more financial information must be secured. He asked, in conversation, 'Are we to divide the tax-field or the tax-yield?'. It is a problem familiar in the discussion of federal constitutions, such as that of Canada, where services are shared out between federal and provincial legislatures. In July 1950 McNeil appointed a Committee on Scottish Financial and Trade Statistics, chaired by Lord Catto. Before it reported in 1952, the Labour government had fallen, the Covenant organization had suffered splits, and public interest had subsided. The S.N.P. had in 1948 altered its constitution to exclude members of other parties. During the 1950s only the Scottish Liberal Party, led by Jo Grimond, did much to concert a Home Rule campaign. The Unionists appointed in 1952 a Royal Commission, chaired by the Earl of Balfour, to review the arrangements for exercising the functions of H.M. Government in Scotland, which reported in 1954 in favour of slight further administrative devolution. But it stressed the need for recognition that Scotland is a nation and voluntarily entered into union with England as a partner and not as a dependency.

Scotland's economy fared ill in the Churchill and Eden administrations, and, after the loss of Conservative seats at the 1959 election, Harold Macmillan accelerated a policy of Scottish industrial development. But it was too little and too late to stop a massive swing back to Labour, which in 1966 reached its record of 46 out of the 71 Scots seats, the Liberals taking five. Further, from 1962, the Scottish National Party took a new lease of life with the emergence of a younger generation of leaders. At a West Lothian by-election the Tory and Liberal candidates were easily beaten as runners-up to Labour by William Wolfe, a local industrialist, who is also a chartered accountant and had been a popular Boy Scout leader. He rapidly built up a model constituency organization. Another young activist, Iain Macdonald, airman and farmer, took over the national organization and increased S.N.P. membership from about 2,000 in 1962 to over 130,000, in over 500 branches, in early 1969. At the Hamilton by-election, in November 1967, 46 per cent of the poll won victory for Mrs. Winifred Ewing, a charismatic Glasgow lawyer, with a quick wit, a sharp tongue, and an I.L.P. background, which helped her to win over some 40 per cent of those who had voted Labour in 1966. At the municipal elections in May 1968 the S.N.P. gained 100 seats, taking about 30 per cent of the vote in the four cities, and the 21 large and 59 small burghs where elections are fought with party political labels. In May 1969 the S.N.P. had a further net gain of 20 seats, and took 23 per cent of the poll. In Glasgow the S.N.P. share fell from 35·5 per cent to 27·5, but still somewhat exceeded the Labour share.

It is possible that the revived S.N.P., with its predominantly young membership, is replacing Labour today as the main radical force in Scottish politics, as Labour replaced the Liberals between 1922 and 1924. On recent form, at a general election in 1970 or 1971, the S.N.P. might win a dozen or so seats, perhaps even 40 out of the whole 71.

The *Glasgow Herald*, in its 1969 *Trade Review*, observed: 'In politics, the London domination of Scottish affairs has been rudely shaken and there can be little doubt that the trend will now be towards greater self-determination. It is only to be hoped that this will stop short of separatism.' The next Tory government of the

United Kingdom might accept a massive nationalist vote as a mandate to implement the principle of Labour's Government of Scotland Bill of 1927, and remove the Scots and the Welsh to legislatures of their own. In 1964 it was the Scots and Welsh Labour majorities that made Harold Wilson Prime Minister over an English Tory majority. England, and especially English Conservatism, has nothing to gain nowadays, strategically or economically, from having Scots and Welsh at Westminster; and appreciation of this fact may well grow as fact-finding and discussion proceed about the claims of Scotland and Wales to equality of rights among the nations, and the consequences of their implementation.

Philosophically, if there are to be nation-states at all, it is hard to see why Scotland and Wales should not have equality of rights of self-government among the world's nation-states, however limited such rights ought to be in the interests of world peace and international trade. As the English nation is renowned for its sense of fair play, it seems to be an insult to England for Scotsmen or Welshmen to demand for their own nations anything less than the degree of national sovereignty that Englishmen would naturally assert for the self-respecting English nation.

2

Aspects of Nationalism

ROBERT McLAUGHLAN

There is a class of word much beloved of political theorists—and practitioners even—which defies definition, or at least agreement as to its precise meaning. 'Sovereignty' is a conspicuous example. But there is another class of far greater import, endowed with a potency which comes from a far more popular appeal, yet remaining obscure; indeed gaining strength and romantic association from its ability to avoid being pinned down. 'Race' is such a word and 'nation' is another. Both are words with a long pedigree. 'Race' seems first to have been used in English by the Scots poet, William Dunbar, in a poem of 1508 and, curiously enough, the first recorded English use of 'nation' is also in a literary context—A Medieval Poetic History of the World, *Cursor Mundi*. But each owes its plausibility to an association with nature and in the modern usage was coined anew in the latter half of the eighteenth century when races and nations began to be invented.[1]

The study of race has often been associated with science—sometimes spurious, sometimes methodologically inadequate—but the study of nationalism has tended to be confined to historians who have until recently preferred to study nations. Now that political science is more developed, nationalism is receiving closer scrutiny and historians themselves, particularly students of 'Third World' history, are investigating its morphology.[2] But the problem

---

[1] The persistence of the association with nature may be seen in Konrad Adenauer's protest to the Russians that 'the division of Germany is abnormal. It is against human and divine law and against nature' (*New York Times*, 10 September, 1955), quoted in Rupert Emerson, *From Empire to Nation*, Harvard, 1960, p. 431.

[2] Some used to think it was disappearing as a contemporary phenonemon. See, for example: 'Nationalism shows signs of having exhausted its strength except among the most backward peoples.' J. Holland Rose, *Nationality in Modern History*, London, 1916, pp. 152-3. A feeling that nationalism would be in retreat after the Second World War was also common; see Barbara Ward, *Nationalism and Ideology*, London, 1967, pp. 12-13.

which confronts them is immense because the nationalist myth is total; there exists cultural nationalism, religious nationalism, economic nationalism, and so on. The core of the myth is none-theless political. Nations are held to be natural or divine creations. They are groups of people sharing a common experience and an 'awareness' of their corporate identity (nationality). Experience and identity alike insist that such groups make their own political decisions within the compartment of political geography which they recognize to be their nation. Where the facts of political geography are incompatible with the establishment of such a polity the facts must be changed.

Because it is the sense of identity which is crucial to the creation of a national consciousness, it is obvious why nationalism has proved to be a major political solvent. Its devotees' consciousness can be triggered by anything—language, race, religion, or simply historical mythology—and the result is almost always a demand for a distinct national state. In building this state the creative energies of nationalism are displayed, but the process is seldom pleasant, since those who do not share the nationalist drive are held to be national enemies and suffer various degrees of rejection and victimization accordingly. The recent spate of 'quisling' notes in Scotland is a local example of this fact, but history abounds with others; the Ashanti in Nkrumah's Ghana, the Ibos in Northern Nigeria, the East European Germans since 1945, the Balkan minorities after the First World War, the Boer collaborators and defeatists after 1900 in South Africa.

These experiences seem almost inevitable for, at least in the process of achieving self-determination, and often in the sub-sequent consolidating and expansionist phases, the nation must recognize no divisions either social or political. Where divisions exist they must be submerged in the national interest. And where members of the nation fail to recognize their identity as part of the nation they must be coerced. Treitschke's view of the need to incorporate Alsace-Lorraine in 1871 overrode any right of the inhabitants of the provinces to dissent to their incorporation: 'We desire, *even against their will*, to restore them to themselves.'[1] Bismarck, Treitschke's hero, was significantly opposed to the

---

[1] Hans Kohn, *Nationalism: its Meaning and History*, New York, 1955, p. 61 (my italics).

acquisition of the provinces, but eventually accepted the military arguments of the General Staff.

It is this supremacy of the national interest which allows nationalism its ideological independence, as it were. It would seem that nationalism is compatible with any of the world's prevailing ideologies. John Stuart Mill, for example, fused nationalism and liberal democracy: 'It is in general a necessary condition of free institutions that the boundaries of government should coincide, in the main, with those of nationality', a view held with disastrous results by Woodrow Wilson and the national self-determinists in 1918.[1] The Greater German nationalists were not to be found amid the Junker class from which Bismarck came but among the liberal intelligentsia; and the focus of their national pride was not the army with its aristocratic high command but the high seas fleet, officered mainly by the bourgeoisie. Chinese communism is now seen to embody a more successful nationalism than did the Kuo Min Tang,[2] and Afrikaner nationalism reigns triumphant in a capitalist economy dominated by foreign investment and English-speaking South Africans.[3] Russian nationalism is now equally obvious—and obviously involved in the space race; so is American.[4]

If current ideology is unimportant in either encouraging or inhibiting the growth of a national consciousness, the same cannot be said of history. A history would seem to be indispensable to the nationalist. And where the history does not exist it has either to be invented or adopted. Even where it exists it has usually to be adapted, so that ultimately all nationalist history is spurious to

---

[1] Quoted by David Thompson in 'The Changing Meaning of Nationalism', *The Listener*, 14 June, 1962.

[2] See C. A. Johnston, *Peasant Nationalism and Communist Power; The Emergence of Revolutionary China 1937–1945*, Stanford, 1963; particularly Chapter 7 which compares Chinese and Yugoslav Communism. Johnston concludes that 'Popular Communism without a basis in nationalism does not exist' (p. 179).

[3] Afrikaners used to think this financial dominance was what they partly were struggling against, but they have learned to live with it. See E. S. Munger, *Afrikaner and Afrikan Nationalism*, London, 1967.

[4] Russian nationalism was evoked by the German invasion in 1941 and deliberately stimulated by Stalin. See R. W. Pethyridge, *A History of Post-War Russia*, London, 1966, p. 24. However, the spirit of Soviet nationalism may be identified earlier, for example in the Red Army's switch from 'internationalism' to 'defensism' in the late thirties. See John Erickson, *The Soviet High Command*, London, 1962.

a greater or lesser degree.[1] The re-emergence of names from Africa's past to launch new states is a minor example of this trend. Dr. Nkrumah's Ghana had only the most tenuous (trading) connection with the medieval West African empire of Ghana which was situated hundreds of miles to the north and west. (More conspicuous examples of Dr. Nkrumah's historical inventiveness are to be seen in Accra, where murals depicted Ghanaian achievements from the past, including the discovery of the wheel.)

Adoption is no less evident and national history everywhere testifies to it.[2] Adaptation—re-reading and -writing the history of the past few centuries in the light of nationalism—is less common, but evident. Indeed, among what may be termed the Anglophobic nationalisms—Scottish, Irish, French Canadian, and Afrikaner—the first is unique in having no substantial nationalist historiography. Such a historiography might have had a beginning in the works of someone like Agnes Mure Mackenzie or earlier with Evan McLeod Barron; but the general weakness of Scottish historical studies, which persisted until very recently, probably prevented the emergence of such a school. So did the fact that nineteenth-century Scotland had many of the things nationalists elsewhere wished to achieve: its own Church, in an age when religion was held in greater esteem than now; its own educational system, then universally held in high respect; and its own law. What more was needed but a parliament, the lack of which may not have seemed so important before the great waves of Irish immigration in the latter half of the century, when the General Assembly of the Church of Scotland still seemed like a National Assembly?

Nor did Scotland have cause to feel threatened by the English as did the French Canadians, the Boers or the Irish. There was no English aristocracy of any note in Scotland and no English settlement (although there are now nearly a quarter of a million English- or Welsh-born living in Scotland).[3] On the other hand,

---

[1] An interesting attempt to study the role of national bias in Anglo-American history textbooks is to be found in R. A. Billington, *The Historians' Contribution to Anglo-American Misunderstanding*, London, 1966.

[2] For example, the way in which nationalist histories have adopted the history of ancient empires covering the same geographical areas. Ancient Egypt's role in Pan Africanist writing is a case in point.

[3] See H. J. Hanham, *Scottish Nationalism*, London, 1969, p. 49.

even a Liberal like Lord Durham wanted to deprive the French
Canadians of their separate identity—for their own good! 'It is to
elevate them from that inferiority [French Canadian Nationalism]
that I desire to give to the Canadians our English nationality.'[1]
Durham despised the French Canadians much as Milner despised
the Boers and most Englishmen the Bog Irish.[2] It is little wonder
that the French believed that the union of Upper and Lower
Canada proposed by Durham was intended to encompass their
ruin and sought to make it instead an instrument to perpetuate
their distinctions[3]—a policy which has proved markedly successful, even if they remain unsatisfied. In the case of the Boers, they
responded to the challenge of political and cultural extinction
(Milner was to add racial swamping) by creating a new language,
refusing to compromise politically with the British, and re-writing
their history in terms of nationalist myth as a conscious device to
promote national solidarity.[4] None of this was necessary for
Scots.

Because they did not have a distinct language or a religion which
was threatened and they did have their own distinctions protected
by the Treaty of Union, Scottish nationalism has always been
more a cultural than a political phenomenon. Anglophobia is
present in some Scottish historical writing and (at one time) in
history teaching in schools, but it has never been taken seriously
either by teachers or pupils and has certainly never been significant
in the universities. A very marked contrast is to be found in
Afrikaner historical writing. There history is still almost entirely
dominated by the nationalist myth in a racist context. Afrikaner
historians who have broken loose are a tiny, if distinguished,
minority.[5]

There is another reason why Scots did not produce much of
a separatist political nationalism in the last century: the aspirations

---

[1] Sir C. P. Lucas, ed., *Lord Durham's Report*, London, 1912, vol. 11, p. 292.

[2] An interesting example of this contempt for the Irish is to be found in the
first edition of *Oliver Twist*, where Dickens expressed the view that the Irish
were 'generally the lowest orders of anything'. He excised the passage from
later editions. See K. Tillotson, *Oliver Twist: a variorum edition*, London, 1966,
p. 49.

[3] See the views of Louis Hippolyte Lafontaine quoted in J. Schull, *Laurier*,
Toronto, 1966, p. 14.

[4] L. M. Thompson, 'Afrikaner Nationalist Historiography and the Policy
of Apartheid', *Journal of African History*, 3, 1962.

[5] See Thompson, loc. cit.

which nationalism satisfied elsewhere were met by the opportunities and success of the Empire. That greater stage which
nationalists nearly always sought in creating bigger political units
was already vouchsafed to Scots, and they made the most of it.

They did produce all the bogus trappings of nationalism, like
national dress, an anthem and a flag, a new national drink even;
but they did not produce a contemporary national leader. The
Führer Prinzip, or at least a line of heroes, is almost essential to
nationalism. It is very evident in contemporary Afro-Asian
national movements, but even Cavour and Bismarck, emphatically
not nationalists, were quickly claimed as national heroes and
unifiers. Compared with such cynical diplomatists, the only modern
Scottish hero, Robert Burns, is significantly in a cultural context,
even if it be one drained of much of its vitality by sentimentalism.
Apart from Burns, Scottish heroes are hard to find without going
back to Bruce (an immigrant, or immigrant's offspring, to use an
Enoch Powellism) and Wallace. Even the Scottish intellectual
tradition from its lad o' pairts to its commonsense philosophy was
unfriendly to the nationalist myth, for it countered it with another:
that of 'the democratic intellect'.[1] There was no metaphysical
tradition in philosophy and politics to take the Scots down the
road followed by so many others. There was—and has been until
the last few years—a great gap between the minority which
achieved a sense of national consciousness and the majority which
either did not, or did not feel it was important enough to bother
about politically.

The one positive role which nationalism might have been
expected to play—that of unification—was not required in
Scotland. When Professor Hanham says that Scotland has had
'all the characteristics of a distinct nation since the twelfth
century', he really means that Scotland approximately attained
her present boundaries at such an early date.[2] But even in the case
of countries which were cultural or geographical units, like
Germany and Italy before unification, it is doubtful how far
nationalism produced unity. In this respect its role is at best
ambiguous for, of course, in defining who should be included in
a nation—which is an entirely arbitrary judgement—others have

---

[1] This is a myth because it clearly runs contrary to much of the Scottish
experience which is markedly authoritarian.

[2] See H. J. Hanham, *Scottish Nationalism*, London, 1969, p. 49.

to be excluded, or if included reduced to an inferior status. It is not hard to document these points. Even after 1871 a Germany which did not include the Catholic Austrians (Germans, too, as a real nationalist like Hitler insisted) was unsure of its unity. There was always talk of its fragmentation. Today the existence of Herr Franz Joseph Strauss's Christian Social Union with its power confined to Bavaria is a reminder that separatism still exists in a relatively mild form after nearly a century of political union. In Italy it has been necessary to grant autonomy to Garibaldi's great prize, Sicily, while the inhabitants of his other conquest, the former Kingdom of Naples, often find themselves treated like foreigners when they migrate to the richer north.

The inferiority of, and discrimination against, minorities within a nation is quite a significant point since, in spite of all the talk about internationalism, a trend which runs from Mazzini to contemporary Scottish Nationalists, it is hard for the nationalist to recognize the claims of competing nationalities, or ungrudgingly admit the existence of minorities and their rights. Czechoslovakia between the wars is an outstanding exception here, but examples of the main point are legion. Kossuth refused to recognize the rights of the Croats just as completely as President Kenyatta refuses the nationalist aspirations of Kenya's Somalis. Tribal nepotism in sensitive areas like the allocation of scholarships, the provision of public utilities, and the awarding of contracts was a marked feature of Nigerian life before the present civil war and seems widespread in other parts of Africa. A list of suffering minorities would be formidable; so would a list of those who believed themselves to be suffering, whether or not the grievance was obvious to outsiders: the French Canadians now and the Sudeten Germans in the 1930s readily spring to mind.[1]

The sense of deprivation exists because the sense of national identity is widespread but seen to be incapable of complete fulfilment. It is this stage, the leap from consciousness to action, which has hitherto been lacking in Scotland; and it is a leap that is essential to political nationalism. There are several distinct stages in the march of nationalism. Each leads naturally to the

---

[1] Though Lord Durham thought 'The English population will never tolerate the French pretensions to nationality' (Lucas ed., *Report*, gloss on p. 59), the French have nevertheless maintained that nationality, and it hardly seems threatened now.

B

next, but not ineluctably—nations can suffer infanticide. Though he later confessed his 'error', Gladstone was quite right when he recognized that the South had become a nation during the American Civil War. But it did not survive; nor, it seems, will Biafra, although its national identity is real enough. Groups may acquire a sense of national identity without insisting on achieving national sovereignty, which is the position in which most Scotsmen, and Welshmen, have found, and continue to find, themselves[1]. The first stage is now pre-packed, as it were: the whole concept of nationality is established as part of the facts of political life. This, the achievement of the French Revolutionary and Napoleonic era, saves a great deal of thought. It is a reminder that the nation is a premise to be assumed, not a fact to be observed.

For nineteenth-century nationalists this was not entirely true. Individuals did struggle a bit with the concept of nationality. If it was Rousseau who first identified 'people' and 'nation', and the revolutionaries who saw that 'nation' was a more appealing word than 'state', associated with *Ancien Régime*, to describe the political community,[2] it was the work of several isolated intellectuals which gave popular substance to the idea of nationality, although their initial work was not politically separatist but cultural and cosmopolitan. Herder is the outstanding representative of this group and it is typical of his lack of narrow appeal that his influence was at least as profound among Slavs as Germans.

These early writers, like Herder, were reacting against the cultural dominance of France. For a time, under Napoleon, this dominion of the mind was coextensive with the French *Imperium* but it had been established earlier. It is probably a mistake, therefore, to see the origins of European nationalism in the military reaction to France. It was the threat France posed to cultural identity and integrity which originally stimulated other European intellectuals. France from the reign of Louis XIV was the greatest Power in Europe. She was the most populous, the best administered, the richest both culturally and materially. French was the language of the *haut monde* and of diplomacy. It was also the language of ideas. Consequently the French were

---

[1] In this respect the United Kingdom may be likened to a successful Hapsburg Empire.
[2] See K. R. Minogue, *Nationalism*, London, 1967, Chapter 2.

supremely self-confident, a position which can easily become arrogance. The revolution deprived the French of the crown as a focus of loyalty. They invented and substituted *La France*, (significantly with 'natural' boundaries), the tricolour, and the Marseillaise. But this, the first stage of nationalism, was no conscious movement—it was spontaneous, hence its lack of definition.

If a new French consciousness and the earlier European reaction to French cultural hegemony produced the first flowerings of nationalism, the second stage, its spread to the bourgeoisie, is more vital. This bourgeois awareness is the starting point for all nationalist movements since the idea became explicit in the years before 1848. It is this awareness which has widely spread from Europe ever since, so that if nationalism is the doctrine of the young it is also that of the middle- and especially the lower-middle-classes, whose role it is to recognize that the poets, philosophers, and students of folk-lore have established the fact of national existence and that this existence is threatened, or its fullest expression denied, by the prevailing political structure. France played in Europe the role she was later to play in Morocco and Indo-China; the role Britain, or people of British descent, were to play in India and South Africa—that of threatening to destroy the cultural integrity of existing societies. The kind of nationalism thus evoked may often have some of the qualities of a cultural defence mechanism, but it very quickly acquires political overtones as it is more widely disseminated.

Once the sense of identity is transferred from the few to the many, nationalism enters a new stage and acquires a new dynamic: what Holland Rose called 'an aggressive and intolerant instinct'. It is this phase in which it is most optimistic and youthful, enjoying an immense fund of enthusiasm of almost crusading intensity, open to manipulation by acknowledged national leaders demanding self-determination or the realization of the national destiny. In this stage too, nationalism is at its least rational and most emotional: significantly it is at its most powerful and persuasive. The nation now has a distinct personality, a psyche, an *amour propre* which is acutely sensitive and easily insulted. Indeed it may be that in some cases a sense of nationalism is to be related to a deep sense of insufficiency. The upsurge in Russian nationalism after the humiliation of the Crimean War springs to mind. So does the stridency of German nationalist demands between the political demise of Bismarck and the outbreak of war in 1914; Germans demanded 'a place in the sun' to which they were *entitled* but deprived of by greedy (more successful?) rivals. Scottish nationalism may have something of this element, too, in the way in which, for many, England has become a convenient scapegoat for Scottish failures or deficiencies.

Since the war, British nationalism has not found a more intensive expression than during the Suez episode which resulted in a total defeat and which itself followed the long retreat from Empire and the growing dissatisfaction with the Commonwealth as an effective substitute. The recrudescence of Scottish nationalism may be dated from this period, when it became obvious that membership of the United Kingdom had lost much of its attraction with the decline of England, the dominant partner, as a factor in world affairs. However, a sense of nationalism has remained alive in both countries and certainly in England, where the Conservatives retain many of the characteristics of an English nationalist party. The way in which they reserve to themselves the use of the national symbols, for example the flag, a technique which none of their rivals emulate, and their long-term lack of appeal both in Scotland and in Wales lend this observation a weight which cannot be ignored. They are more prone, too, to the spirit of national intolerance as exemplified in attitudes to immigrants to the United Kingdom. Although this spirit is by no means confined to Conservatives, it seems significant that, both in the case of Jewish immigration at the end of the last century and coloured immigration in this, it has been Conservative politicians who have articulated, if not stimulated, the fears of the natives—all the while seeing themselves as guardians of the national character.[1]

Nationalism produces unstable situations even when triumphant and established. In small states it is least aggressive, since by definition they can have few pretensions harmful to the general peace. But even in such states a highly developed sense of national identity can produce acute problems; Flemish national sentiment is a case in point and, of course, the Spanish Civil War was in great measure a struggle between the competing nationalisms of Castile and more peripheral areas like Catalonia and the Basque

[1] See John A. Garrard, 'Parallels of Protest: English Reactions to Jewish and Commonwealth Immigration', *Race*, lx, i, 1967.

provinces. (It is the contrast between this purely Spanish concern and the basic irrelevancy of the international conflict of Communism and Fascism which supplies the war with a tragic dimension.) On the larger scale the demands of nationalism and the national interest have gradually proved themselves unacceptable to liberal thinkers, until the present position is one where nationalism is not a respectable intellectual position to hold; which may be why liberals keep predicting its demise. The fate of Mr. Dubcek's Czechoslovakia and, earlier, Mr. Nagy's Hungary at the hands of Russia is eloquent testimony to the continuing power of a sense of national interest in determining Russian policy in Eastern Europe. And the same considerations, although even more irrational, have long prevented the United States from putting her relations with Red China on a reasonable basis. Indeed, a safe generalization would be that nationalism has made the conduct of international relations everywhere more difficult since national public opinion, fragile and febrile as it is, always remains ready to feel slighted. Diplomatists must long for a complete return to that secrecy so much decried by E. D. Morel and other radicals after the First World War.

Though the greater part of liberal opinion would share these views, liberals are not entirely consistent in their dealings with nationalism for it clearly confronts them with a dilemma—as may be seen in the case of the Scottish Liberal Party, which alienates some support because it leans too close to the nationalists and yet alienates the nationalists because it does not lean closely enough. The dilemma is most acute in the case of the post-war triumph of nationalism in the Afro-Asian countries, for there nationalism is, as it was at an earlier stage in European history, closely intertwined with democracy, with freedom, and the sanctity of majorities. European liberals have been conspicuously involved in that process and have generally supported the demands for national self-determination, although it often has had the effect of Balkanization as, for example, in the cases of India, Indo-China, and French West Africa.

Nationalism, although a European invention, could not be confined to Europe. Indeed it was, often unconsciously, promoted by Europeans, whose missionary and cultural efforts in the Middle East, Africa, and India produced new élites schooled in European techniques but kept in a state of inferiority owing to the presence

of European military power. In most of these countries an independent professional middle class was a new phenomenon: it
was also therefore young. Its sense of deprivation was real and the
whole nationalist case found a receptivity long before the end of
the nineteenth century. This century has seen the success of
Afro-Asian nationalism perhaps because of the decline in European
self-confidence (and effective military power) but also because the
rise of modern mass media of communication gave the nationalist
élites an audience which was denied to the pioneers of nationalism.
It may come as a surprise to some to note that the cry 'Africa for
the Africans' is almost a century old and that the idea of an
'African personality' was first discussed in South Africa in the
1890s, that Pan-Africanism is to be dated even earlier, and Arab
nationalism earlier still. For Africans this cultural nationalism was
a protective mechanism whereby they sought to accept European
technology but retain their own sense of identity from the stifling
embrace of Western religion and education, an embrace which was
always half-hearted since Europeans were seldom willing to accept
the possibility of complete assimilation. This cultural phase
eventually flowed into the more militant Pan-African movement,
which has proved a non-starter simply because in most cases the
second stage of African nationalism involved appeals to existing
communities with a strong sense of identity—the tribes. (Tribal
nationalism is the source of the present Nigerian war, although
ironically those who were swiftest to abandon tribal for a wider
Nigerian identity, the Ibos, have proved to be the war's most
conspicuous victims.)

If one asks why such a political doctrine capable of only the
most vague formulation has proved—and clearly continues to
prove—so appealing, there are clearly two reasons. Human beings
desperately want to belong to a community which is respected, a
community where membership confers a sense of privilege and
possibly of power. This is why nationalism, although it may be
born of a sense of inferiority, is seldom characterized by modesty.
In the second place, it is a powerful force because it is essentially
Utopian, promising total freedom, complete self-expression—
usually hitherto denied—and happiness. (Thinking along these
lines it becomes obvious that the contradictions in national
socialism are more apparent than real.) It is because of this
totality, this refusal to admit that men are in fact everywhere

divided by economic interest, social class, religion, ideology, temperament, or what you will, that nationalism is to be classed as a great instrument of tyranny disguised as a noble sentiment. And this has been its historic role, however much contemporary nationalists in Scotland and elsewhere may protest. For the political nationalist would seem destined to open a Pandora's box. Violence may be first out, but its ensuing companions will be no less ugly.

3

Scottish Nationalism, Law, and Self-Government

T. B. SMITH

The title of this chapter as first suggested by the Editor was 'Scots Law and Scottish Nationalism'. Its proposed theme was to be the relevance of Scots Law in the event either of complete Scottish independence or of the establishment of a federal form of government. On reflection, however, it has seemed to me that 'Scots Law and Scottish Nationalism' is a theme related to, but not co-extensive with, the consequences for the Scottish legal system of basic constitutional changes. This chapter will therefore discuss both themes and their interrelation.

'Scots Law and Scottish Nationalism' is a phrase which is charged with emotion—and this indeed provides a useful point of departure for the present essay. Even the most dedicated lawyer, if he moves much in the world of men and women outside his profession, is well aware that lawyers present to the layman a double image (one of which is highly unfavourable) while, like a drainage system, law itself tends to attract lay interest only when it obviously works badly. It may be doubted whether exhortations to draw freedom's sword for the Scottish legal system would have stirred to self-sacrifice the average Jock or most of those who led him in 1314 or 1940. On the other hand, a reflective Jock in 1940 might well have resented the fact that, when he put on the kilt in his king's service, he subjected himself to a 'British' military law and procedure which was expressly and entirely English, and in many respects inferior to Scottish solutions. As in so many other contexts, 'British' meant 'English'; and against an accumulation of such pinpricks Scotsmen tend to react in irritation—often without a very clear idea of what the Scottish position may be.

When Lord Belhaven, in his celebrated speech on the eve of the Union, lamented 'I think I see *our learned Judges* laying aside their Practiques and Decisions, studying the Common Law of England, gravelled with Certioraries etc.', he did not direct his mind to the fact that in the preceding quarter century Stair, under pretext of restating the law of Scotland, had in fact—with the aid of Continental jurisprudence—formulated for the first time a coherent system of Scottish private law. Meanwhile Mackenzie had performed a similar service in the field of criminal law. The great achievement of these Scottish jurists was to have made cosmopolitan and systematic what had been largely inarticulate. They had a proper pride in the law of Scotland, but they were also concerned to present it as participating in a Western European tradition—the *ius commune* from which (English law excepted) individual national systems then diverged only to a limited extent.

Scots law in the seventeenth and eighteenth centuries was not a subinsular and intolerantly nationalist system (like the English common law). It was a synthesis drawing extensively on foreign legal ideas, and was formulated and adapted for application in Scotland by a few judges and jurists of wide interests and experience. The factors which since the first half of the nineteenth century have to some extent corroded Scots law in its administration and intellectual content have been a curious combination of complacency and lack of self-confidence in developing the system, resulting in a tendency towards parochialism.[1] Scots lawyers may look over their shoulders to check how problems are solved in England; but they seldom now look further.

Against this background one may consider current 'Scottish nationalist' attitudes to 'Scots law'. Can Scottish law—in substance and administration—be regarded as an aspect of the Scottish national ethos? Some, including the late Lord President Cooper, and on a lower plane and in a more limited sense the present writer, believe that it was and could be again. On the other hand, it is important not to exaggerate. There is something unconvincing about certain theories of 'legal nationalism' which treat a nation's laws as a mystical by-product of a national ethos. Savigny and his followers believed that through a *Volksgeist* each people developed

[1] See T. B. Smith, 'Legal Imperialism and Legal Parochialism', 1965 *Juridical Review*, 39.

its own legal habits much as it developed its own language and other aspects of culture; while, as law and life became increasingly complex, the lawyer had to become the mediator and interpreter of the *Volksgeist*. Among the more absurd and unreal interpretations of a *Volksgeist*—that of England—one may cite Sir Frederick Pollock's vision of the English common law in 1912. He described 'Our Lady of the Common Law' as belonging 'to the kindred of Homer's Gods, more powerful than men; not passionless or infallible, she can be jealous with Hera, ruthless with Artemis, and astute with Athene. We are her men of life and limb and bodily worship.' (None, it may be added, outside England have been voluntary converts to her worship; and the English layman who frequents her shrines leaves few votive offerings.) Many euphoric postprandial speeches have been delivered by eminent persons on 'The Scottish Legal Tradition', but none which attained the Pollock level.

I am sceptical of genetic jurisprudence. Scots law in its classical era was the achievement of professional lawyers and of the Lowlands, though Sir George Mackenzie could in a sense be regarded as a Highland contributor. Emigration and immigration have altered substantially the racial composition of Scotland's population since the classical era. However, the Savigny theory that lawyers in time become the mediators of a country's legal and cultural attitudes suggests that it may be helpful to distinguish between the 'nationally-minded' Scottish layman's views on his country's laws and the views held by Scottish lawyers on the same subject. To some extent, of course, these are interrelated, because the layman may have listened to the lawyers.

The layman is seldom interested in the details or technicalities of legal science, though he will resent examples of manifest injustice of the law in action. The Scottish layman may well resent the lack of a Scottish legislature, or the second-class treatment of his legal system by the legislature at Westminster (as by imposing United Kingdom legislation in English form, and by denying Parliamentary time for Scottish measures) or obvious and ill-considered anglicization by case law. He will incline to support 'his law' as he would support 'his country' at Hampden Park or Murrayfield, though if he is a commercial man he will be irritated by technical differences between Scots and English law in mercantile matters. From what he has read or observed of some

Scottish lawyers in action he may well regard the country's legal system and its practitioners with only qualified esteem—compared, for example, with the Scottish medical profession which enjoys an exalted reputation at home and abroad. However, the Scottish 'nationalist' probably regards his country's laws as providing better safeguards for fair trial and personal liberty than does England, and believes that the Union Agreement provides fundamental protection for these and for basic Scottish institutions, including the law. The first of these beliefs is probably well-founded, but the second is not. A few general comments may be offered on the 'nationalist's' romantic attachment to the Union Agreement. In some ways, like Magna Carta (which was not much concerned with the common people), it has been invoked as a slogan in inapposite situations and has, moreover, like the Charter, been mythologized.

The complex of documents which constitute the Union Agreement have a threefold significance. In the first place they constituted a treaty in international law, concluded, not by the Scottish and English Parliaments, but by Anne, Queen of Scotland, with Anne, Queen of England. This treaty was executed on 1 May 1707 and is no longer a source of binding mutual *international* obligation. The former states of Scotland and England ceased to exist in 1707, and a new state or person recognized in international law replaced them. Next, the Acts of the pre-Union Parliaments operated as ordinary legislation only within the respective jurisdictions. Lastly, the Union Agreement took effect as skeletal, but nonetheless fundamental, law for the new Kingdom of Great Britain when it came into being. The third aspect alone has contemporary relevance.

Three notable omissions from the basic constitution are apparent. First, though the Articles of Union are careful to protect every aspect of the Scottish Establishment in the early eighteenth century, they make no provision for the protection of the rights or liberties of ordinary Scotsmen and Scotswomen. The Union Agreement is therefore no palladium of liberty, and differs from later written constitutions of the eighteenth century which were concerned with the rights of man.

Secondly, no machinery is provided for amendment of the basic constitution, an omission which had to be faced in time, though Irish rather than Scottish affairs probably stimulated the more ridiculous English doctrines of Parliamentary Sovereignty. Nevertheless, in fact the only two clear cases of Westminster legislation irreconcilable on strict construction with the fundamental Articles were instigated by Scottish interests.[1] From shortly after the Union, London governments were sensitive about legislating upon purely Scottish affairs, especially if such intervention might seem to be inconsistent with the terms of Union. The assumption of greater initiative by London governments to impose legislative solutions on Scotland dates from the early nineteenth century, in response to agitation by Scottish Whig lawyers who wished to bring Scotland 'within the constitution' (that is to say what they believed to be the advantages of English institutions), and after conservative Scots lawyers had mismanaged the reorganization of the Court of Session.

Thirdly, no provision was made for judicial or other scrutiny of legislation which might conflict with the basic constitution. Even had such provision been made, it would have been of little avail to the ordinary citizen, who could seldom establish title to sue in respect of interests protected by the Agreement, except under Article XVIII in respect of laws concerning 'private right', which is today a more restricted field than in the eighteenth century. Though the Union Agreement did not make express provision for judicial 'policing' of legislation inconsistent with the constitution, this in itself would not have precluded judicial intervention. The Supreme Court of the United States assumed such a role *ex proprio motu*.[2] A more serious theoretical difficulty concerned separation of powers. In the early eighteenth century the House of Lords was an important legislative chamber and also (with the same membership) the ultimate court of appeal for Scottish and English civil causes; while until 1733 Senators of the College of Justice in Scotland could and did sit as Members of the House of Commons.

In short, it may be concluded that the Scottish 'nationally-minded' layman has put too great a faith in the Union Agreement to protect Scots law concerning individual or national interests.

---

[1] *Scil.* the reorganization of the Court of Session and the removal of the religious test imposed on Principals and professors in the Scottish Universities. See generally Smith, *Studies Critical and Comparative*, Edinburgh, 1962, p. 14; N. T. Phillipson, *The Reform of the Court of Session 1785–1830* (unpublished thesis), Cambridge, 1967, p. 251.

[2] See especially *Marbury v. Madison*, 1 Cranch 137 (1803).

He has, moreover, seldom had the technical knowledge to realize that expressions like 'the *Treaty* of Union' or '*the* Act of Union' are inaccurate and misleading. Even Scots lawyers of great experience like Lord Cooper have been misled. The lesson to be learnt is that Scotland (or the United Kingdom, for that matter) stands in need of a basic written constitution or constitutions containing provisions for amendment and judicial review; and providing specific protection for human rights including a remedy (perhaps an extended form of the *actio popularis*) to enable the individual to challenge acts of the Legislature and Executive.

The attitude of contemporary Scots lawyers to their legal system and their profession is an important consideration in assessing the likely consequences for law in Scotland of fundamental constitutional changes. It must be suggested with regret that since about the mid-nineteenth century Scots law and the Scottish legal profession have been in an age of decline, though less calamitous than Cockburn feared. I do not imply that Scotland has lacked lawyers of first-class ability, but rather that the system itself lost to a considerable degree its former coherence of principle and flexibility. The leaders of the legal profession, moreover, have ceased to be regarded as the country's élite as their predecessors had been; and they lack the remarkable genius to create law from principle and expound it convincingly, which earlier generations of Scots lawyers possessed. Even so, there is probably a higher standard of professional integrity among leading Scots lawyers today than in the legal profession of any country. Paradoxically, the Union itself did not adversely affect the Scottish legal system. Indeed, the classical era of Scots law is to be found in the late eighteenth and early nineteenth centuries. The eventual decline reflected a more general decline in Scottish culture.

A quotation from Lord Cooper summarizes the background:

> Twice over—first in the thirteenth and then in the seventeenth century—Scotland constructed a legal system out of imported ideas, and on both occasions the work was done with a sturdy independence of outlook. From first to last the effort was to attain simplicity, flexibility and directness, and to attain these things systematically. . . . The forgotten architects of our system . . . were all possessed of the same qualities—self-reliant, severely practical, invincibly logical and with a metaphysical bent. . . . When at long last they had completed their task in the early nineteenth century, they had furnished Scotland

with what most comparative lawyers will agree was an admirably finished philosophical system well in advance of its times.[1]

This system, it may be added, had until the early nineteenth century its closest affinities with the civilian systems of Western Europe. Coherence was provided by the major institutional treatises of Stair, Erskine, and Bell. The impact of English law was negligible. Important legislation for Scotland, though promulgated at Westminster, was considered by the freeholders and by the legal profession in Scotland, and was drafted by the Scottish Law Officers. Though the House of Lords was almost overwhelmed in the late eighteenth century and early nineteenth century with Scottish appeals, the Lords' decisions had little impact on the content of the law itself.

Space forbids a detailed digression on the social history of Scotland, but it is suggested that the decline of Scots law as a system deserving of Lord Cooper's eulogy can be explained only in terms of social history. The close relationship between law, culture, and society in Scotland has now been analyzed by Dr. N. T. Phillipson[2] and Dr. Nan Wilson.[3] They provide an explanation for the rise and fall of the legal profession in national life. The Union of 1707 was made to work in Scotland, despite ultimate control from London, through the Faculty of Advocates. Edinburgh's Golden Age, the Age of Enlightenment, had as its focal point the Parliament House, the seat of the higher Courts.

By 1850, however, Parliament House had become 'little more than the rump of the Enlightenment'.[4] Aristocracy, intellectuals, and young men of ambition had increasingly deserted the northern capital, the universities had declined in esteem, the middle classes were becoming increasingly anglicized, Parliament House had lost much of its self-confidence and its leadership in the national life. From about the same period may be traced a jurisprudential decline, partly manifested in the emergence of a prickly parochial-

---

[1] *Selected Papers*, 1922–1954, Edinburgh, 1957, pp. 178–9.

[2] Phillipson, op. cit.

[3] Nan Wilson, 'The Scottish Bar: The Evolution of the Faculty of Advocates in its Social Setting', *Louisiana Law Review*, 235, 1968; 'The Faculty of Advocates Today', *Acta Juridica* 1965–6, p. 227; and *The Sociology of a Profession: The Faculty of Advocates* (unpublished thesis), Edinburgh, 1965.

[4] Phillipson, op. cit., p. 345.

ism and in an increasing tendency to anglicize the *content* of Scots law. These attitudes seeped from the centre to the circumference of the legal system. Contributory factors to the partial undermining of the Scottish legal system were the legislation passed to deal with new developments in the economic and social life of Britain as a whole, and the activity of Scottish Whig lawyers who strove and succeeded in their endeavour to bring Scotland 'within the constitution'. Phillipson has well expressed the paradox of their achievement:

> Their reforming programme had been directed towards including Scotland within the Constitution, by which they meant the bestowing upon their fellow-countrymen of the same sort of liberties that were enjoyed by Englishmen. . . . They realized that liberties could only be obtained at a price and that was the progressive elimination of the institutions, customs and manners which had characterized the life of Scotland as an independent country.[1]

Ironically, probably their major struggle was to secure civil jury trial for Scotland—an institution which the English have now in their wisdom largely discarded.

Busy lawyers cannot be constantly concerned with jurisprudential excellence, and it has always been a few intellectual leaders who have given a 'style' to a legal system. Lord Cooper observed that much legislation had:

> no better title to be recognized as an integral part of our system of jurisprudence than the current issue of the railway timetable. Accordingly, when we speak of a legal system, let us think rather of the body of principles and doctrines which determine personal status and relations, which regulate the acquisition and enjoyment of property and its transfer between the living or its transmission from the dead, which define and control contractual and other obligations, and which provide for the enforcement of rights and the remedying of wrongs.[2]

In a contemporary setting, though much legislation deserves Lord Cooper's description, increasingly the central principles and doctrines of a system will be altered or enunciated by Act of Parliament and ultimately codification will provide the basis for

[1] Ibid, p. 343.
[2] *Selected Papers*, p. 174.

judicial decision. However, the Lord President defines appropriately (apart from public law) the main areas of a legal system which are relevant for the formation of a lawyer and by reference to which the quality of a country's laws may be judged.

The most distressing feature of present legal attitudes in Scotland is neglect of the intellectual content of Scots law—its systematic coherence and its basic principles—in the search for precedents to provide a short cut to the solution of problems. A clear indication of vitality in any legal system is a flourishing legal literature as an auxiliary to legal development. Twenty years ago Scottish legal literature had come close to drying up, apart from a few manuals charting somewhat uncritically case and statute law. Within the last ten years a few dedicated men have—especially under the auspices of the Scottish Universities Law Institute—endeavoured for minimal reward to provide comprehensive treatises on the main divisions of the law in Scotland. Their labours have received disappointing recognition by the legal profession, which has shown itself reluctant to purchase and ready to criticize, especially the cost. For a small country legal literature is necessarily expensive—but other small countries pay willingly. Though there is deep concern for the independence and prosperity of the Scottish legal profession, there is no obvious general professional concern for Scots law as such. Except in limited areas, which concern financial interests, law reform as an adjunct of social reform does not greatly involve practising lawyers, and it may be thought that there is less support in Scotland than in England for the work of institutions such as the Law Commissions which were established in 1965.

The need for brevity has compelled over-emphasis and over-simplification. For over a century a few individuals have arisen in each generation who have seen Scots law as Lord Cooper saw it, and who have wished to re-establish its pristine excellence. Some have been so moved emotionally as to cherish even the anomalies and anachronisms of Scots law because they are Scottish. Noting that the main disintegrating force has been the impact of English law, they have reacted furiously against all English legal solutions. By contrast, in the era when Scots lawyers were confident in their system, there was no disposition to be hostile to any legal system provided that its solutions were not imposed on Scotland uncritically and by pseudo-comparative processes.

My own view, as a disciple of the late Lord Cooper, is that in many areas the harmonization of Scots and English law by joint endeavour to improve both is desirable. Parity of negotiating power and genuine comparative methods are essential. Even if Scotland achieves independence or federal self-government, it is to be hoped that any development of her law in the future would take account of English jurisprudence as of that of other legal systems of similar economic, social, and political conditions. Nevertheless, at the present time, it is suggested, a sense of 'otherness' with regard to English law is not necessarily to be deprecated. As in South Africa and Quebec, so in Scotland, such an attitude may be an indispensable preliminary for uncovering the true foundations of a national system, based on the civil law, which needs to discard excrescences of uncritically imposed or imported English law. It is probable that with important exceptions such attitudes are to be found more among a few leading judges and university law teachers than among the practising profession. This is readily understandable. After all, it is the primary function of legal scholars and the higher judiciary to safeguard the essential merits of a legal system and to develop it in response to contemporary conditions. Planning is the province of commanders and staff rather than of the regimental officer who is in the smoke of battle. It cannot, however, be claimed that in 1969 the interest of Scots lawyers in general is greatly aroused by wider jurisprudential considerations affecting the legal system which they operate.

Such an assessment of attitudes towards law and the legal profession in Scotland is an essential preparation for considering the prospects for each in the event of a basic constitutional change—whether that takes the form of federalism or of independence for Scotland. (The solution of 'regionalism' is discarded as quite unsuitable for an equal partner in the Union of 1707 which still retains such basic institutions as an independent legal system.)

Political independence tends to produce intense legal activity in constitutional matters, and the Scottish legal system would necessarily be supplemented by an important new apparatus of public law (excluding criminal law which is on the whole satisfactory). It is much less likely that there would be comparable endeavour to alter the structure of private law or those legal techniques which determine how law is in practice applied to the

solution of problems and disputes. Though it is apparent that
Scots law could be improved on many issues, there is no consensus
as to how it should be improved. The Scottish National Party
does not seem to have strong views on questions of Scottish
private law. It is also reasonably clear that the legal profession,
trained in and accustomed to certain legal techniques, which have
already been mentioned, have no strong desire to change them.
The drift from principle to precedent and restricted methods of
statutory interpretation characterizes Scots law in action today.
Scottish legal scholars would certainly hope that greater control
of Scots law by Scottish lawyers would result—either through
case law or by legislation—in the purging of the system of irrelevant
or inhibiting English doctrines. These are most apparent in the
fields of obligations or moveable property, fields where English
law, when relatively undeveloped, was influential and inhibiting on
a more mature Scots law. It would seem better policy today, if
research resources and legislative opportunity are provided in a
new constitutional structure, to restate the main areas of private
law in modern codified form than to seek to reinstate in patchwork
fashion the classical law as such. On the other hand, it cannot be
urged too strongly that the policy should be *more maiorum: usu
hodierno*—unless, as in family law, for example, traditional attitudes have become irrelevant. What is probably most worth preserving and developing in the law of Scotland is that area of
private law which attracts little publicity and occupies relatively
little judicial time, but is the basis of the Scots lawyer's training. To
a layman it may seem strange that so small an area—compared with
the vast and complex jungle of 'laws'—should be so important.
One may suggest the analogy of language. The quality of a
country's language and literature cannot be assessed by reference
to the volume and content of all that is presented in print. A Scots
lawyer, like a French lawyer, should be concerned with the 'style'
of his system, which is largely set by the structure of private law.

    Were self-government to be restored to Scotland, the challenge
of outstanding importance, from a legal standpoint, would be the
working of a constitution. Since the Union, the law relating to the
central executive power and to Parliament has been essentially
English, and the country's external affairs have been conducted as
those of England. If Scotland had again complete political
independence, Scots lawyers would have to apply themselves with

urgency to problems of public international and supranational law, from which they have been virtually excluded for over three and a half centuries. Thus ancient skills have faded through disuse. The external representation of Britain—even before 1707—has been controlled from London; and the image of the United Kingdom has consistently been distorted to reflect England and English interests. English Law Officers and legal civil servants advise the governments of the day on international obligations, and only within the past five years or so has any Scottish lawyer participated in the discussion of international conventions. Were Scotland to become a state again, she would need to find lawyers capable of coping with the wide range of international legal problems which would result. An immediate consequence of independence would be to negotiate interdependent relations with other states, including, presumably, important treaty relationships with England. At Edinburgh University, at least, there is a nucleus of experts who could advise and train in the complex specialist international law field. If, however, Scotland acquires some federal form of self-government, it may be predicted that London will generally continue to project abroad in legal and diplomatic contexts the image of the United Kingdom as England. When differences between Scottish and English law are relevant, greater weight may possibly be given in external relations to Scottish legal opinion than has been the practice in the past. Moreover, the developing practice of the United Kingdom government consulting the Scottish and English Law Commissions on certain draft international conventions would presumably continue.

Independence or devolution of powers within a federation would necessitate the re-establishment of a legislature in Scotland. Since the Union took effect the Westminster Parliament has never served Scottish needs adequately. Today, reasons for dissatisfaction and recognition of them are more widespread than ever before. Parliament is too much concerned with too heavy an English-orientated legislative programme and with too many problems concerning external relations to devote adequate time to the consideration of Scottish problems. Indeed, among the world's legal systems Scotland has shared with the District of Columbia the dubious distinction of having a separate legal system without a separate legislature to regulate it. Moreover, the two-party system as represented at Westminster does not reflect contemporary

Scottish opinion, which, on the whole, is more radical and dissatisfied than is the English electorate—the dissatisfaction cutting across more general 'British' social and economic patterns.

A Scottish Parliament in Edinburgh would be free to legislate for Scottish needs and in particular to devote adequate time to law reform—including the simplification, modernization, and codification or consolidation of the main divisions of the law. This would, of course, be an onerous and continuous task as well as a great opportunity. The work of the Scottish Law Commission has already resulted in a number of urgent proposals for law reform which have not been implemented because of lack of parliamentary time at Westminster. Any Scottish Government would need to allocate very substantial sums for work on law reform if the Scottish legal system is to be restated in accordance with its basic principles and with the needs of the late twentieth century.

Much would depend on the interest and initiative of Scotland's Government in legal matters. Within the present constitutional structure, legislative policy for Scotland and its implementation are inhibited by executive as well as by legislative considerations. The impact on a government of a Lord Chancellor intent on law reform—such as the Earl of Birkenhead or Lord Gardiner—is apparent in matters of English law. Even so, English lawyers periodically urge the desirability of establishing a Ministry of Justice, as in other countries, with a minister responsible for law reform and the improvement of the legal system generally. The Secretary of State for Scotland is seldom himself a lawyer, and cannot be expected to have these objects among his priorities when he is responsible for so many other aspects of government policy affecting Scotland. Nor can the Lord Advocate, whose duties combine distinct and not necessarily complementary functions, effectively assume the role of Minister of Justice for Scotland. A consequence of fundamental constitutional changes in Britain should be the establishment of the equivalent of a Ministry of Justice with primary responsibility for the legal system and its satisfactory functioning. This might be achieved by reorganizing and expanding the Department of Lord Advocate, the appointment of an additional Law Officer, and the recruitment of an adequate staff of draftsmen and legal experts. Under a federal solution, it would be essential for the minister responsible for Scotland's legal affairs to have a much more effective voice than at present regarding such legislative policies of the central government as would affect national and international interests.

The restoring to Scotland of responsibility for and control of legislation might, however, create in her lawyers (including those serving in the Government) a new spirit of enthusiasm for reform, and alter dramatically the average lawyer's attitude, which is somewhat redolent of parochialism and complacency—but also tempered at times with uncritical deference to English law. A study of the world's legal systems seems to indicate that modernization and comprehensive restatement of any legal system depend on self-confidence and the spirit of reform among those who direct a nation's affairs. The impetus—as in the case of the early nineteenth-century codifications—may, of course, be provided from outside and in opposition to the legal profession. Or again, there could be an avatar in the tradition of Stair or Cooper to inspire the preparation and eventual legislative promulgation of a traditional, but cosmopolitan and contemporary, Scots law. It is, however, not at all impossible that in Scotland as in other countries emancipated from Westminster, much legislation would continue to be based on London fashions. If uniformity or harmonization of law is to be promoted, this practice within limits is not objectionable. It is, however, important for Scotland that harmonization by legislation should also take account of developments in jurisdictions which are not derived from English law.

Next must be considered the contribution of the judiciary in the event of independence or of devolution of legislative and executive powers within a federal structure. Very important new responsibilities would probably be vested in the higher judiciary in particular, and for these responsibilities they and their successors for a generation have had neither training nor experience. It would presumably become the judges' duty to 'police' the constitution, and to restrain the Executive and Legislature from exceeding their appointed powers. Interpretation of a constitution, which would be basically a written document, demands techniques beyond those required for the interpretation of ordinary legislation, if undue rigidity is to be avoided. Within the present constitutional structure the judiciary has rarely, if ever, seriously considered checking the powers of Parliament and has been reluctant to restrain acts of the Executive when it is armed by Parliament with wide and often indeterminate powers. It may well be that a special jurisdiction to deal with matters of administrative law at all levels should be established.

A new constitution whether federal or independent would, it is hoped, include express provision for the safeguard of human rights, for which no provision was made in the constitution of 1707. The judiciary would have the duty of protecting these rights within the constitution, and would therefore have the opportunity to develop the rule of law in situations where the balance between public and private interest is most delicate. In addition to assuming these new duties under the constitution, the judiciary would, of course, continue to exercise its established functions. If, as may be hoped rather than predicted, the establishment of a legislature in Scotland provided the impetus and opportunity for extensive legislative law reform—including codification and consolidation of important branches of the law—the success of these measures would depend largely on judicial interpretation. So far Scottish judges have not had to develop, as have their counterparts in Europe and elsewhere, techniques for the interpretation and re-interpretation of codes in their modern sense. In developing the existing common law of Scotland, the Scottish judiciary might no doubt feel less inhibited if the Court of Session were to be the final court in civil cases, as is the High Court of Justiciary in criminal matters. Independence would exclude appeals to the House of Lords, but a federal solution need not.

The House of Lords, before and after the appointment of Scottish law lords, has undoubtedly corrupted and distorted sound Scottish civilian legal principles by interpreting the problems in English juristic terms. Relatively few practising lawyers, however, are concerned with *elegantia iuris*. Moreover, some Scots lawyers today (like the Cockburn school of Whig advocates) consider that the intellectual calibre of the judges in the House of Lords greatly excels that of the average Senator of the College of Justice; and conclude that even the possibility of appeal is a stimulating and restraining influence on certain judges. Under a federal solution it is thought that the majority of practitioners in Parliament House— though not necessarily in Scotland as a whole—would wish to retain the right to appeal to the House of Lords or equivalent United Kingdom tribunal. Such a court might well become the ultimate arbiter of constitutional questions including conflicts between 'national' and 'federal' organs of government.

Leaving aside the future role of the House of Lords as outside the scope of this essay, would independence or federalism affect substantially the law as administered in the Scottish courts? Unless Scots law is set within a wider European framework, it may be doubted whether there would be any dramatic change. The role of Scots private law generally—obligations and moveables in particular—might well have been to mediate between Civilian and Anglo-American systems. No grand ambitions can now be entertained realistically. Scots law, if its basic concepts are sufficiently revealed and developed, may yet, however, in the drafting of codes and conventions, influence harmonization of law in Britain and in Europe. It must be stressed that the securing of a measure of uniformity of laws within the United Kingdom is desirable, and the securing of uniformity or harmonization of laws within a wider context—Civilian and Anglo-American—is also ultimately desirable, though speedy and dramatic results are not anticipated. Legal nationalism in the sense of parochialism is to be deplored. The work of the present Scottish and English Law Commissions takes account of unification and harmonization as desirable objectives. At various levels lawyers of many countries are seeking for greater uniformity in the administration of justice, especially where, as increasingly happens, legal problems transcend frontiers—as in the sale or transport of goods or a vehicle accident on a family holiday abroad, or death, marriage or adoption in a foreign country.

It is important to realize that lawyers provide a service for the adjustment of human relationships—economic and personal. A fundamental constitutional change would not necessarily affect extensively the present balance of economic control of Scottish mercantile and industrial concerns. In this book such matters are essentially within the province of Professor Alexander and Dr. Simpson. However, when considering future legal developments in Scotland, a lawyer cannot ignore the fact that the commercial and financial predominance of England in Britain must necessarily influence the course of development of Scottish mercantile law. Nevertheless, it may be observed that English law is itself under pressure to conform to wider international patterns, and Scottish industry is not restricted to English sources for capital investment. In an era of standard-form contracts and mass production of goods and services, juristic frontiers can usually be evaded or demolished. In the public sector of economic activity, it is apparent that the headquarters of the 'nationalized' corporations such as the 'Bank of England' and the 'National Coal Board' are invariably established in England and ensure a London-based Government's control over administration or redistribution of British assets. Here again the policy decisions which will affect the relevant law in Scotland will continue (under a federal solution) to be made without regard for possible inconvenience for the country's legal system. In short, in the economic sector of national life the pressures will be opposed to divergence from English law —though it may be accepted that Scots law can play a useful part in rationalizing a substantially United Kingdom mercantile and industrial law, for example in the field of contracts, especially of sale.

Political emancipation might stimulate a confident creative upsurge among the lawyers of Scotland, but immediate manifestations are not to be expected. Professor J. J. Gow in the preface to *The Mercantile and Industrial Law of Scotland* has written:

> In this exceedingly complex society of ours, what the lawyer dare not be without is a knowledge of the economic, political and social facts of his civilization. He needs this knowledge not as a dilettante, not even as a matter of personal cultivation, important though that may be, but as a matter of professional competence. There is no law in the sky; it is the ever-recurring manifestation of man's intelligence, skill, and moral values. No legal profession is entitled to rely on obsolescence. In the past (i.e. from about the mid-nineteenth century) the inability of successive generations of Scots lawyers to master their contemporary social facts and hazard intelligent conjecture of future facts has done much to impair the efficiency of our legal system. The immediate cause of this inability was lack of proper legal education.

This harsh diagnosis unfortunately seems justified, and a constitutional reorientation of Scotland would make even more essential the need for a Scots lawyer to master 'the economic, political, and social facts of his civilization'. The future of law in Scotland therefore would ultimately depend even more than at present on governmental interest in law reform, on the work of the Scottish Law Commission, and on the teaching and inspiration of Scottish university law faculties, which are seriously under-staffed, especially in respect of the heart country of Scots law.

In the twenty-first century the judiciary, the practising profession, the Scottish Law Commission and the law faculties themselves, may be manned by a new generation of Scots bred in a
freedom denied to their forebears. It could be that in such a
changed political climate a new confidence will grow. Confidence,
as Sir Kenneth Clark has discerned, is the clue to civilization; and
law is an aspect of civilization. It may be that imbued with a new
confidence born of opportunity and responsibility, Scots law will
again make a contribution to law—free from parochial and pseudo-
comparative inhibitions and in the philosophical and comparative
tradition of the Classical era.

4

Independence and Constitutional Change

NEIL MacCORMICK

Scottish independence may be seen as a means to an end or as an end in itself. To see it as an end in itself is to adopt a very pure nationalist principle: simply because Scotland is a nation, she ought to become a separate state. Under that principle the only question for argument is whether Scotland is indeed a nation. To accept pure nationalism, however, one must accept a variety of metaphysical beliefs about the nature of nations, beliefs about which rational discussion can scarcely be conducted; one takes pure nationalism, or one leaves it. For my part I leave it, and shall say no more of it here.

A utilitarian nationalism, on the other hand, is concerned to propose independence as being the best means to the well-being of Scottish people. That is a proposal about which rational argument can, and should, be held. The context in which I shall discuss it here is the context of constitutional reform. An awareness of the processes of constitutional change which would be involved in making Scotland independent is essential to an enlightened appreciation of the arguments for and against independence, or such more modest reforms as federation or devolution.

As a first step in this discussion I wish to set out briefly what seems to me to be the central and essential argument upon which the utilitarian nationalist case depends. It is that Scottish society is at present a sick society because it lacks a democratic political centre, specifically responsible to the Scottish electorate for tackling Scottish problems and determining Scottish priorities. Parliamentary democracy does not involve the electorate directly in solving problems, but it does enable them to participate in settling the broad priorities, and to accept them willingly by virtue of their own responsibility for them. In a modern state it is evident that the radical social and technological changes which have been accelerating over the past fifty years must be to a large extent regulated and implemented by government; a modern state is necessarily an interventionist state. But this produces in a community such as Scotland a sense that these changes (whether good or bad) are outside the control of its members, which inhibits constructive discussion or willing implementation of change. Whatever one dislikes can be pilloried as an alien intrusion. The cure for this sickness is to create an independent centre of political life in Scotland to take control of Scottish affairs. The energies of a highly educated community (which sees itself as a community) can only be harnessed if its members are, and know they are, responsible for their own common destiny.

In short, the centralization of political and economic power round the centre of government, which necessarily characterizes modern states, makes it necessary to diversify centres of government. Centralization in its present form will reduce Scotland to the worst sort of provincialism and parochialism, unless a real centre of political power is established in Scotland. This argument is more fully deployed in other essays in this book, so I can be brief. The point is that independence would restore to Scots people a sense of responsibility and, much more important, the *reality* of responsibility for their own future. That would create the opportunity for a real release of energy in this run-down community, to the great benefit of its whole culture and economy. It would staunch, if not reverse, the brain drain. It might even bring the Scots to solve their problems rather than blame them on the English.

It is, of course, generally accepted that Scotland and Wales are industrially run-down, and correspondingly socially depressed areas, as indeed are many areas of England. But regionalism in its present form appears a self-defeating cure since it involves the enlargement of central government powers and influence in the economy—that is, greater centralization—with a view to remedying the ills which are in large measure due to over-centralization. It smacks of homoeopathy further to fatten the leviathan in order to cure the sickness caused by its already excessive size. Real economic and social improvement in Scotland will depend upon local initiative, and that the present climate stifles.

Of course, this is necessarily a nationalist argument in a fairly obvious sense of the word, though as the essays in this book show, it is not the sole property of the Scottish National Party. It depends essentially on the proposition that people in (geographical) Scotland are on the whole conscious of themselves as forming a distinct community with a distinctive tradition and culture, embodied in and protected by such separate institutions as their educational system, legal system, church, and languages. Historically, this community as a self-conscious unit may not have been so homogeneous socially or culturally for so long as is sometimes suggested. But the fact is that most Scots now regard themselves as belonging to a community of respectable antiquity, and wish to preserve its distinctiveness (whether or not they are political Nationalists): and that is the fact that matters.

The argument which I have sketched out seems, as I said, to be the central and the most persuasive one which can be adduced in favour of independence as a means to an end; and it is one which I find convincing. But as a utilitarian argument, it is subject to two very important and very obvious limitations. First, it does not appear to be conclusive in favour of independence as such. It makes out an extremely strong case for creating a centre of real political power in Scotland. But it does not show that the greatest benefits would necessarily be achieved by creating a totally separate state in Scotland. The same argument can be, and is, used by those who advocate devolution of power to a Scottish Parliament, or federalism in Britain. Secondly, the utilitarian case for independence forces us to take into account the disadvantages as well as the benefits to be expected, which brings in the economic debate and all the considerations of defence and internationalism, and the risk of losing by fission the very real values of the British way of life: traditions of tolerance and freedom, and so on. It is upon considerations of the latter kind that the debate between devolutionists, federalists, and separatists turns, the debate being concerned to establish which form of government would secure the greatest benefits at the least cost. It is possible, no doubt, to opt out of that debate by the bare assertion of the pure nationalist principle, that all nations must be states though the heavens fall. But that principle is not one about which worthwhile argument can be conducted, nor does it seem to command widespread assent.

Upon this view of the matter, the vital question of principle is not whether Scotland should become wholly independent or not. It is whether or not we shall choose to establish *some* form of separate political institutions in Scotland, and shall take a pragmatic and utilitarian view in deciding which form would be most beneficial. The fundamentally opposed alternative is to insist on preserving the present unitary system of government in Britain, whether or not it is harmful to the minority nations as such.

That in itself does not, however, dispose of the need to choose what form of government should be adopted for Scotland; nor does it mean that the differences between the various live possibilities are in any sense trivial. But I do believe that the nature of the choice can be made clearer by considering in outline the constitutional changes open to us, and by examining the processes by which these changes would have to be made.

The live possibilities are of course devolution, federation, and independence within a customs union. Of these devolution involves the least change, since the present Parliament in Westminster would retain its present degree of sovereignty over the whole Kingdom. Domestic parliaments would be created in Scotland and Wales and possibly in the provinces of England, as a logical extension of the Redcliffe-Maud Commission's proposals. Such parliaments would have control over executives responsible for discharging a limited range of functions within the area concerned. But in constitutional theory and in practice the powers of such parliaments would merely be delegated powers, to which the U.K. Parliament might add and from which it might derogate entirely of its own motion; it could even abolish them if it saw fit. A critical question would be what sort of financial powers such parliaments should have; necessarily, they must have power to spend money, but should they have any power to raise it? If they have none, they remain very much under the thumb of the central government, on which they depend for grants; if they have the sole power over direct taxation, there are difficulties over redistribution of wealth from richer to poorer areas, and the central government is perhaps excessively weakened. Any intermediate scheme means that the citizen is twice taxed by two (expensively maintained) bureaucracies.

Devolution of this sort can, of course, be applied *ad hoc* to those areas in which there is real demand for local home rule. It already works in Ulster, and Scotland or Wales could be added without necessarily disturbing the mode of government of England. But on the Ulster model there is a serious problem, the question of representation in Westminster. Northern Ireland has at present half as many M.P.s in Westminster in proportion to its total electorate as do the other parts of Britain. This is rather illogical, since, so far as U.K. politics are directly relevant to Northern Ireland, that area should not be under-represented; while it should not be represented at all where matters solely affecting the domestic affairs of the rest of the United Kingdom are concerned. But in our system of government, governments must have working majorities for all purposes, as they would not always have if Ulster M.P.s were excluded for some purposes, and included for others; whence the rather odd compromise. Very few Scots, however, would appear to desire a domestic parliament if the cost were reduction of their representation in a Westminster Parliament charged with taking decisions of major importance for Scotland.

Of course, if there were to be at the same time a radical devolution of power to provincial governments in England, that problem would disappear. But there is not yet strong demand for that, though there are good arguments in favour of it. The question, therefore, is whether or not Scotland (and Wales) should wait until there is; and whether they would, in any event, find it satisfactory to have parliaments with powers no greater than are desired for the provinces of England.

A fortiori, federalism would also eliminate the problem of England's being governed by the Celtic fringe while having no power over the fringe's domestic affairs; and the alternative problem of Scotland or Wales being under-represented like Northern Ireland in the central parliament. A federation would necessarily involve dividing the Kingdom into units; but unlike devolution it would entail a rigorous division of powers between central and local governments, with judicial supervision of that boundary. There would be a United Kingdom Government with a stated range of powers, and Welsh, Scottish, and English (or English provincial) parliaments with powers over all other matters.

(Alternatively, on the Canadian rather than the U.S. model, stated powers might go to the provincial parliaments, with residual powers, only in part specified, left to the federal parliament. On the whole, the U.S. model seems preferable.) The constitution would have to be written as a whole, and would be unalterable save by some complex procedure requiring the cooperation both of federal and provincial (or 'national') parliaments.

Thus federation goes further along the road towards independence, in that it divides sovereignty between U.K. and provincial parliaments rather than leaving the central parliament in the last resort supreme in every field. It may, therefore, better protect local parliaments against erosion of their powers—though it is evident that federation has not prevented a very great degree of centralization of power at the federal level in the U.S.A., for example, over the past fifty years. Nevertheless, the advantages in such a system of giving real autonomy to states or provinces are considerable; that it involves judicial review of legislation for constitutionality, conveys the further advantage of facilitating the entrenchment of citizens' fundamental rights against legislative erosion.

The converse disadvantages are that federal constitutions are necessarily inflexible and hard to change; that they lead to multiplication of judicial and administrative hierarchies; and that the processes attendant upon judicial review grow into an extensive and expensive, but unproductive, light industry. Moreover, there are special difficulties in making a federation work in which one of the units is, in terms of population and total wealth, very much greater than the others; and England is in such a position in relation to Scotland, Wales, and Northern Ireland. It seems unlikely that English people would want to make areas of England into partly sovereign states, though they might swallow devolution all round.

An appreciation of all the difficulties involved in devolution or federation has led some to suggest that the only simple and workable answer would be to carve the U.K. into separate states wholly independent of each other, their sovereignty limited only by supranational arrangements mutually negotiated. That limitation is significant, since the official policies of the S.N.P. and Plaid Cymru advocate the negotiation of a customs union among the British nations. This policy has not been fully elaborated, but it must be said that a customs union necessarily involves common political organs among its members. The obvious example of this is the European communities with their complex structure of political institutions. A common market is necessarily a political and legal unit, however loose. Indeed, we must take note of the widely held opinion that in Europe the road ahead leads either towards dissolution of the communities or towards increased political fusion including a *directly elected* European parliament. If the European analogy is to be pressed, independence in a customs union may be a course which would bring us back towards some kind of federation. But be that as it may, there would in the short term be a significant difference between some kind of loose confederation of independent states in Britain,[1] and the two alternatives discussed. Moreover, there is something in the argument that in our circumstances it would be simpler to work.

Those, then, are the possible courses between which one who accepts the argument about the benefits of greater Scottish autonomy in government must choose. The choice seems to be a bewildering one. How can we judge with any precision which course would be most beneficial and least harmful? Argument is currently raging over numerous variations on the themes outlined, yet all the arguments turn upon wildly divergent assessments of imponderable probabilities.

But the argument must be put in its practical setting: the process of constitutional change which would be involved in creating a Scottish Parliament and Executive. It is impossible to know *a priori* which of the courses proposed would really be best for everyone, though of course we need to elaborate and examine the best case that can be made out at present for any proposal. I wish to suggest as the final and the essential point of this essay that independence would have to be preceded by devolution, and that this fact vitally transforms the debate.

Suppose that the people of Scotland voted overwhelmingly and unequivocally for independence; suppose that the English majority in Westminster resolved to bow to their desire. Even in those circumstances it would be impossible to establish a separate Scottish state overnight. At this moment Scotland does not have

---

[1] The usage of the term 'federation' and 'confederation' which I follow here is based upon Sir Kenneth Wheare's (K. C. Wheare, *Federal Government*, 4th ed., Oxford, 1965). It differs from that adopted by David Steel. See below p. 86.

the necessary governmental machinery to constitute a viable state. Certainly a Scottish Parliament could be set up fairly quickly. Once elections were held, a ministry could be formed by whoever could command the necessary support in that Parliament. But a ministry needs machinery of government, and that does not exist. The departments of the Scottish Office (Home and Health, Agriculture, Education, and Development) exist as self-sufficient units, and various U.K. ministries have Scottish regional offices. But there is no separate Scottish Treasury, or Foreign Office, or Defence Ministry, or Board of Trade, or Department of Employment and Productivity, or Ministry of Technology,[1] and so on. Yet all these are agencies without which an independent Scotland could not function. In particular, a Treasury is the essential nerve-centre of a working state, which must raise money by taxation and oversee its expenditure from some central point. It would not be short work to unscramble the British Treasury into national components so as to establish an independent one in Scotland.

Defence is another obvious example. How do you split up the British forces, and distribute the military equipment? Only after long negotiation, to say the least. A similar problem arises with the nationalized industries. How do you divide their assets and liabilities, and how quickly can you constitute Scottish Boards to run the new Scottish state industries? Another set of problems centres on sharing out existing financial assets and liabilities—the division of pension funds and maintenance of pension rights, the division of the national debt (who owes what to Scottish holders of British Government stocks?) and so on.

These are simply examples which illustrate the magnitude of the practical problems involved in separating off a Scottish state from the United Kingdom. The cases expressly mentioned are only the tip of a huge iceberg. To create all the necessary agencies of the new state, and equitably to divide the national assets and liabilities of the present unit is, seen as a whole, a most complex problem. If the constitutional changes were to proceed by way of orderly transition from the existing unitary governmental structure to a structure of separate units, it seems clear that we should have to advance stage by stage. The problems would become manageable if tackled one by one, but what should the stages be?

[1] The names of the latter two are new, but their functions are old and important.

C

Before that question is answered, it is important to make the point that 'orderly transition' is utterly essential for the well-being of the country. Whatever view one takes of the prospective economic strength of an independent Scotland established in favourable conditions, it is plain that economic disaster would be the likeliest consequence of a hasty and ill-considered transfer of powers. Confidence is at the roots of economic well-being. In modern conditions, governmental competence is a necessary condition of industrial and commercial confidence. An independence worked out stage by stage, with an orderly transference of powers from the existing British institutions to newly developed Scottish ones—as and when these are brought into working order and have been seen to be working—would not forfeit confidence. But a hasty and botched-up job could leave a legacy like that from which Eire is only now beginning to escape. That is the critical importance of the question to which I now return: what stages?

Given that there is already a separate legal system (including the Crown Office) and a separate set of departments in the Scottish Office, it would clearly be possible to establish at once a Scottish Parliament to deal with all matters of private and criminal law, and with the whole field now covered by the Scottish Office. The Scottish ministers would be chosen from and responsible to that Parliament rather than the Westminster Parliament. The substantial problem in such an arrangement would be that the income of these Scottish ministries would still be wholly determined by votes of the U.K. Parliament. So the second stage would have to be the creation—still within the U.K.—of some sort of Scottish Treasury, which once it was established could be put under the control of the Scottish Parliament, after the negotiation of a satisfactory system of paying for common U.K. services. This would involve investing the Scottish Parliament with appropriate taxing powers, subject to some suitable arrangement for the payment of what is known in the Government of Ireland Act as an 'Imperial Contribution' towards common services. Thrashing out a suitable formula for this operation of transferring financial powers would of course be extremely difficult. It is the kind of problem which drives some nationalists to believe that the quick clean break from incorporating union to total independence is preferable to a gradual transference of powers. But it is worth reiterating that the former is not a real alternative since we could not reasonably expect to maintain confidence without a well-planned transference of financial and economic powers. It would be quite impossible to create a working Treasury overnight.

Once a Scottish Government and Parliament existed and had acquired a real measure of economic and financial power, the further stages would be reasonably simple. By a similar process to that of creating a Treasury, Scottish departments should be split off from the central ministries; then put under control of ministers responsible to the Scottish Parliament by means of an appropriate extension of the legislative competence of that Parliament. Eventually a stage would be reached at which the Scottish Parliament would enjoy an unlimited competence over all fields. At that stage Scotland would have reached independence. Up to that point, since the U.K. Parliament would have control over some aspects of the government of Scotland, it would be necessary for Scottish Members to sit in that Parliament. This necessity is further reinforced by the fact that the extension of the powers of the Scottish Parliament would be a process which would require the cooperation of the U.K. Parliament—though it would seem sound, and would accord with precedents set in the Commonwealth, that such extensions should be made always and only on the request and consent of the Scottish Parliament.

That the creation of a limited government and parliament would be the most appropriate first step in this process is further demonstrated by the fact that the division of the functions of U.K. ministries, and the splitting up of such things as the assets of the Ministry of Defence and the Nationalized Industries, and of the National Debt, would very obviously call for a good deal of hard negotiation. But nobody would have *locus standi* to negotiate for Scotland until there was some sort of government politically responsible through a parliament to the electorate; so that should be created as the first step in the process.

The Scottish National Party has always affirmed that the desirable method of creating a Scottish state would be by negotiation, and with the agreement of the U.K. Parliament as a whole. But the Party has said that, failing such agreement, the Scottish National members would themselves summon a Scottish Constituent Assembly. Such a course might be justified in extreme circumstances. It can scarcely be denied, however, that this would cause a disastrous upheaval, such as could only be justified by a blank and persistent refusal over a period of time by English M.P.s to yield to the wishes of the Scottish electorate once these had been finally and conclusively ascertained. We should all hope that that will never happen. Collision courses always mean disaster.

It is more constructive to work out what would be involved upon the happier assumption (which I have here made) of English co-operation in setting up an independent Scottish state. In this constructive vein, I have tried to show that a carefully negotiated independence—which the National Party asserts rightly to be most desirable—would necessarily be preceded by the establishment of a limited Scottish Parliament whose powers should be successively extended up to the point of complete autonomy. That is to say, independence would be preceded by devolution. The point can be further reinforced by considering the progress to independence of Commonwealth countries, from direct rule through responsible government, to final independence.

If that is so, however, there is a great deal more common ground between 'separatists' and 'devolutionists' than is commonly supposed by either group. The contribution which a calm appraisal of the processes of constitutional change can make to a constructive view of Scotland's future is that it enables us to be pragmatic in a double sense; not only should we realize that the point at issue between devolutionists and separatists is essentially a factual matter of balancing probable benefits and disadvantages; we should also appreciate that in practice we can work out at any particular stage in the process of increasing Scottish autonomy what the next step should be, and whether it would be wise to take it.

To put the latter point in another way, it is not the case that, if we set out upon a course of devolution with the aim of ultimate independence, we should be unable to stop short of independence. Of course we should be able to, and of course we ought to stop short of independence if at some stage it becomes clear that we have attained the benefits of a real degree of local initiative in Scottish affairs, but that further to extend the process—say by breaking up the unity of British defence policy (a plausible example)—would procure few obvious benefits at a wholly excessive cost. Nor is it the case that a scheme for devolution which did not expressly provide for an advance beyond its framework towards independence either would or could preclude the possibility of such an advance.

At present we are all amateurs trying to work out what this or that course would involve. It should not be forgotten that if any steps are taken towards independence, there will come into existence a government answerable to the Scots electorate at the polls. It seems most unlikely either that such a government would take a step which to its knowledge would have seriously harmful consequences for its electorate, or that it would fail to take obviously beneficial steps. And such a government would be in a position to know the facts as none of us is now.

The immediate course which follows from the foregoing argument is that we ought to try to work out a form of open-ended devolution under which a Scottish Parliament is created with limited powers but with express provision for the unlimited extension of those powers by some stated procedure involving the co-operation of Scottish and British Parliaments. Such an *ad hoc* devolution would probably not be a satisfactory long-term conclusion. It is implicit in all currently proposed schemes that there be some common British machinery of government, either of a federal or quasi-federal, or of a common-market type. The final form of such machinery could best be worked out after practical experience, and once it was known from experience what degree of local autonomy was in fact most beneficial. To work it out we should need to find the opinion not merely of the Scots, the Welsh, and the Irish, but also of the people of England, whose views on all these questions are extremely important but as yet wholly unascertained. The difficulties of *ad hoc* devolution on the Ulster model have already been mentioned. The way round these difficulties is surely by some sort of federation or confederation; which of these it should be is something we should work out in the light of practical experience.

In a book of this kind it seems particularly desirable to see how much common ground there is between varying approaches to the problem. In the midst of all the divergences of opinion and of emphasis which these essays exhibit, there are two threads which seem to run through all. One is an insistence upon the need for co-operation among the peoples of these islands; the other is the need for greater Scottish participation at a local level in Scottish affairs. The advantage of taking a pragmatic approach to our future is that it seems likely to secure both objectives, and in doing so to command a very wide degree of assent; and that is after all the vital element in the working of any constitution. Such a pragmatic approach follows from an appreciation of the realities of constitutional change.

5

Devolution and Local Government Reform

DONALD C. DEWAR

I believe that the structure of government in Scotland will be a major issue in the 1970 election. Perhaps more importantly I believe that it ought to be. Discontent with the present position is real and can be backed by substantial arguments. Misconceptions there are in plenty, but the general impression that the system is fundamentally inefficient can be justified. The real danger is that failure to face the problem, the complacent assumption that this discontent will die, may encourage extreme solutions which can only damage us all.

Throughout the United Kingdom there is a disrespect for government resulting from continuing economic crises and the failure of the parties to satisfy the expectations they themselves have done so much to raise. The electorate is aware of issues as never before and also aware of the government's ability to tackle them. There is no longer a passive acceptance of economic and social distress. The old heavy industrial structure of Scotland has declined—in shipbuilding, in coalmining, and on the railways alone some 90,000 jobs have been lost between 1954 and 1967. The process of contraction has left the debris of Victorian industry sprawled across the country. Reconstruction, though steady, has been slow. Bad housing, high unemployment, low wages are the talk of every politician in opposition. The very nature of the party system ensures that it is these failures which are most forcibly brought to the notice of the electorate.

Scotland is almost invariably compared with England as though the pattern of prosperity was uniform south of the Border. The variations that in fact exist and the evidence of our very real progress can be seen in any issue of the *Employment and Productivity Gazette*, but the sense of grievance remains. S.E.T. is widely thought to have been devised specifically to victimize the hapless Scots despite the heavy weighting in their favour which demonstrably results from the manufacturing premiums and R.E.P. The enormous effort in public spending is there to be seen, but the Secretary of State responsible has gained little credit. In the face of all fact, no less than 52 per cent of those interviewed in a poll commissioned by the B.B.C. in 1968 were convinced independence would improve their standard of living, while only 5 per cent felt that it would suffer as a result. We enjoy—if that is the right word—a great deal of administrative devolution. The bureaucrat, who in popular mythology can be relied on to ride, rough-shod over every local sensibility, almost certainly is to be found in Edinburgh not London. Despite this it is nearly impossible to shake the firm conviction that the enemy is Whitehall and the essential difficulty a matter of geography.

General discontent has been intensified by the continuing tradition of independence which makes Scotland's problem unique in Britain. Plaid Cymru, perhaps too closely identified with the Welsh language to attract really widespread support, does not appear to have maintained its challenge. The S.N.P. in contrast can appeal to all Scotland. The Church, very aware of its distinctive traditions, and the legal profession, jealously guarding its privileges, have helped keep in being a commitment to Scottish concepts. In one poll only 30 per cent of those questioned described themselves as British. Political disaffection is the more formidable when built on such a base.

I am not going to argue the case against separatism. To do so would be to waste time on a policy which can never make sense and which has only the most limited general support. Even full federalism, leaving central government defence and foreign affairs alone, would dangerously fragment co-operative effort in areas where unity really is strength. The United Kingdom is a partnership based on mutual advantage. Independence in the full sense in which it is often used is a myth, the much sought after freedom no more than a sham or, more damaging, the right to opt out of decisions which affect our interests.

One danger is that an over-enthusiastic attack on separatism leads easily to a reaction against all reform. The positive search

must be for a solution on a Scottish basis which will satisfy present
doubts. Local government reform provides an opportunity, but
not in itself a solution. Change must go beyond minor adjustments
to responsibilities and functions or alterations, however sweeping,
to boundaries. The electorate, used to thinking in Scottish terms,
wants to feel that government is more immediately involved in
their problems. There is much talk of participation, but to involve
people in the processes of decision making would demand a commitment to politics few would wish to make. What is wanted is a
system more responsive to public pressure on specific issues and
under which spending priorities are more obviously tailored to
particular Scottish needs.

In parliamentary terms, of course, there is a good deal of devolution at present. Bills relating exclusively to Scotland are normally
discussed both in principle and in detail in Scottish committees.
So far as the English are concerned, such measures appear in the
chamber only for what is often a nearly formal third reading.
Committees must, however, reflect the composition of the House
as a whole, if only to ensure that the government of the day is in a
position to control its own legislative programme. It has been
argued that the presence of English Members on the Grand
Committee to preserve when necessary the administration's
majority should be discontinued and, if a decision unacceptable
to ministers is taken, it should be reversed on the floor of the
House. This would be a concession of no substance, leaving Scots
M.P.s with the power to disrupt, but not rule. Mr. Heath in his
speech at Perth in May 1968 talked in very imprecise terms of a
Scottish assembly which he apparently envisaged as an offshoot of
Westminster removed north of the Tweed. But meaningful
authority, the right to play a real part in the legislative process,
implies the need for a government majority in normal circumstances. This difficulty suggests that a solution must be looked for
outside the Westminster framework.

A fair amount of the criticism of Scottish government reflects
scepticism about Parliament itself. If the Grand Committee is in
one sense a charade, so is much of what takes place in the chamber.
M.P.s have opportunities to influence legislation, but a second
reading debate is not one of these. Only a handful of romantics
imagine a speech is anything more than a propaganda exercise.
But if some regret the inevitable power of the whips, there is every

reason to think they would become a feature of a Scottish assembly in exactly the same way as their influence has increased on most city councils. The Grand Committee on safari in Edinburgh will merely confirm widespread fears and allow the cynics to emphasize the inadequacies of parliamentary procedure in such a way as to suggest these are diseases unique to the Scottish committees.

Released from the tight schedule of an overworked Westminster some of the virtues of the parliamentary system might become more apparent. Adequate time could be found for legislation in important, but less politically controversial, fields such as law reform. The development of a 'Scottish Cabinet' would allow for the more thorough political supervision of the administrative machine. At present the five ministers attached to Dover House must find it difficult to look after the range of topics for which they are nominally responsible. After all in England the same duties are divided among a great number of ministers who do not suffer from the added disadvantage of being stranded some 400 miles from the civil servants whose job it is to implement their political decisions. Even the back-bencher might that bit the more effectively carry out his traditional role as a watch-dog on the executive. At least an opportunity to question those responsible for the bulk of Scottish matters might come up more than once in five weeks. It might even be possible to put down questions in the hope they would be answered when still of some topical interest.

A Scottish tier of government independent of Westminster has other attractions. The growth of a political complex at Edinburgh would in itself be of importance. By creating a range of rewarding and responsible jobs it might do something to hold personnel who would otherwise have drifted south. Good jobs mean congenial company and high salaries—the multiplier effect cannot be ignored. The atmosphere of a capital city is unmistakable and gives some weight to the nationalist argument for the dynamism of independence.

A Scottish administration would on occasions differ politically from that in London. There would be little point in the exercise if it did not. A party condemned to long periods in opposition at Westminster might welcome the chance of holding office in the north and, by providing attractive positions there, utilize the talents of men who would otherwise have been shut out from power. Even today M.P.s moving up from local government clearly miss the executive responsibility they once enjoyed. The role of a back-bencher can become for some an arid experience—particularly when hope is killed by a long period on the wrong side of the House. A Scots administration could attract people of ability and give the chance to build a reputation as even city government today cannot do.

Clearly the all-too-familiar local structure with its inefficient finances and inadequate expertise is about to be eliminated. The thirty-three counties and four cities as we know them are likely to go as reform results in larger units. If this is the trend it would be wise to work on a Scottish framework. One of the difficulties of any new division is the lack of identification with an artificial administrative unit. Scotland, taken as a whole, would start with an enviable reservoir of loyalty and could build on the basis of a continuing tradition. Here the Redcliffe-Maud Report on Local Government in England is of interest.[1] Not that its suggestion of a three-tier structure relying largely on unitary authorities with a population of at least 250,000 topped by a superstructure of eight so-called provincial councils is necessarily right for Scotland. Wheatley is not, nor should be, bound by its decisions. One difficulty is that Maud leaves not only the grass-roots local councils, but also the provinces with practically no defined functions. There is a specific reference to the devolution of central government powers following Crowther, but if the English pattern were to be acceptable to Scotland this would presuppose so significant a shift of responsibility to the provincial administrations as to be almost certainly rejected south of the Border.

We glibly tend to assume that the mood of dissatisfaction so obvious in Scotland is duplicated in the north of England. Disenchantment with government which seems remote, anxiety about centralization, loyalty to distinct regional cultural patterns should be just as marked there. If the case for real administrative centres outside London is accepted, then the needs of York are probably greater than Edinburgh. This may be so, but it is not felt to be so. Despite the widespread abstentions in recent by-elections which many have equated with the Nationalist protest vote, the situations are not comparable. Meetings in England, in my experience, do not sympathize with or in many cases understand the mood in

[1] Cmnd. 4040, H.M.S.O., 1969.

Scotland. The regional parliament is far too radical a departure from accepted practice—conversion would be a lengthy process.

Still the Maud provisions, even if they sound too much like a reconstituted version of the present planning councils, amount to an invitation to establish a Scottish unit of government. The structure would fit the United Kingdom pattern, but the realities of power would be very different. The activities of a Scottish assembly would have to be wider in scope than anything previously allowed to local government. It would, despite what has been suggested for the provinces, have to be directly elected. Democratic control at one remove as favoured by Maud would just not do. It might be more practicable to think in terms of a two-tier structure with Edinburgh taking over at least some of the powers the English report reserves to the unitary authorities. Maud attempts to reconcile efficiency with democracy by leaving local councils to keep in touch with public opinion. Less fortunately he gives them only the vaguest of advisory powers. In Scotland a two-way split might be arranged with personal and social services allotted to a secondary authority of such a size as to allow a live link with the ordinary voter.

However the subordinate structure is organized, a Scottish administration is likely to emerge. Scotland exists in the minds of those who live there and it would be stupid not to recognize the fact when considering the shape of reform. Such a development would provide a chance to simplify the machinery of government. The mass of *ad hoc* bodies which have recently sprung up should be rationalized. The Regional Planning Councils, for example, have had, put politely, only the most limited success with the public. There may be strong arguments against electing their members and equally good reasons for not giving them increased power in their present unreformed state. Their planning functions and the work of that plethora of committees, commissions, and boards set up by central government to serve its convenience could be handed over to the new administration. These, combined with the more important powers of existing local authorities, the administrative functions of St. Andrew's House, and, where suitable, other duties hived off from Westminster, would provide a worthwhile range of responsibilities. There is no reason why law reform or sewage or town planning procedures or water board reorganization should be dealt with in London, as has recently been the case.

But it is not enough to put a democratic foundation under the administrative devolution which presently exists. Once set up the new machinery must have some financial independence if it is to have any real existence. Here the arguments for less ambitious reform become formidable and the implications have to be looked at closely. The method used to allocate public money to Scotland is not easy to follow, but the whole operation is carried through on a United Kingdom basis. The four spending departments which make up the Scottish Office submit detailed estimates to the Public Expenditure Survey Committee as do the British ministries with responsibilities north of the Border. From these a five-year rolling programme is constructed with totals on a functional basis straddling the boundaries between existing departments. When a project included in the key third year survives succeeding reviews it will in course appear in the appropriate programme as an authorized expenditure.

The Scottish share is built up in this way item by item from below and only at a very late stage does a global figure for Scotland emerge as such. St. Andrew's House no doubt has a clear view of their needs and how these can be tailored to fit available resources, but the system does not seem to throw up figures which allow an overall Scottish judgement to be made. Indeed the D.E.A., who laid great stress in their memorandum to the Select Committee on Scottish Affairs on their 'co-ordinating role in respect of both industrial and regional policies', could still when challenged on the Scottish figures admit 'on the whole we do not think very much in these terms'. The Green Paper published in April 1969, *Public Expenditure: a new presentation*, proposes changes which would make a great deal of useful information more generally available, but the criteria on which Scottish totals are based will remain obscure.

The present position is defended simply on the grounds that it works and works well from Scotland's point of view. The system is sufficiently flexible to take account of particular needs and to shape expenditure to meet these. A housing programme, in which in no year since the war has the private sector been responsible for more than 20 per cent of completions, ensures that *per capita* spending in this sector is much higher than in England. The massive emphasis on regional development has resulted in a heavy weighting in Scotland's favour. In a number of ways Scotland

enjoys a particularly privileged position. A United Kingdom
decision may be taken not only as to the absolute public expenditure ceiling, but also as to spending priorities within that
limit. A major effort to improve principal roads may result in the
authorization of a large range of specific projects in Scotland, but
this would not prevent the Secretary of State deciding that a
change of plan was necessary to speed up (for example) work on
the new district general hospitals. In the English planning regions
the decision not to go ahead with certain authorized road schemes
could only mean that the sums saved would drop back into the
national pool for financing such developments. In Scotland, the
Permanent Under-Secretary assured the Select Committee, such
a switch of resources would certainly be possible and this measure
of autonomy is clearly an advantage.

It may be that this fragmented system, which allows hard
bargaining on a number of specific fronts, suits Scotland. Possibly
the final settlement would be less generous if the size of our cut
was to be seen in the form of a simple national total. For all that,
change is a possibility. Maud suggests that even local government
capital allocations should in future be seen in terms of the final
total each authority is to be allowed in the quinquennium as well
as the approximate amounts to be spent in each area of effort. To
do this there would have to be 'central government machinery for
considering each main authority's capital expenditure as an
integrated whole and not by reference only to investment in
particular services'.[1] Scotland's share in future might be based on
an across-the-board agreed total rather than a number of depart-
mental figures negotiated, in one sense at least, in isolation. A
budget, agreed with Westminster and controlled from Edinburgh,
could become reality. That it is compatible with continuing
membership of the United Kingdom is certain and in this respect
a deal might be learnt from the Stormont example. There is an
understandable temptation to write off such a precedent, if only
because the social and political atmosphere is fortunately so
different from that in Scotland. But crippling unemployment and
the bitter sectarian squabbles all too characteristic of Northern
Ireland can hardly be blamed on the financial and administrative
machine. The system evolved is in many ways clumsy, sometimes
downright unlikely, but certainly not without interest.

[1] op. cit., para. 547.

The great mass of taxes are imposed and gathered by the United Kingdom Treasury before being paid over to the Northern Ireland administration. The allocation of these 'reserved revenues' is open to every objection usually raised when the formation of a Scottish public expenditure budget is proposed. The Ulster economy, despite the Irish Channel, is very largely merged with that of the United Kingdom and any division of revenue is bound to be an arbitrary process subject to wide margins of error. Income tax is simply apportioned on the basis of residence, but the yield from customs and excise duties is split in a highly artificial manner with some 2·7 per cent of the United Kingdom total being handed over to Belfast.

The Northern Ireland administration can to a limited extent vary the tax burden at their discretion. The transfer of certain taxes yielding something in the region of 20 per cent of revenue allows a measure of flexibility, but little play has been made with this. The general principle remains that both taxation and the services which the state provides should keep in step with the rest of Britain. Within limits, however, the power to vary could clearly be useful. Items concerned include death duties, stamp duties, and vehicle tax; and on occasions these do depart from the British pattern. Another advantage of the Stormont solution is that it does provide a more workable financial unit. Local income tax might well be a practicable proposition and it should be possible to raise finance more efficiently than the present fragmented structure of local government allows. Some support again comes from the Maud Commission which, although restricted by its terms of reference to local government and its existing powers, stresses the need for financial independence if the type of new authority it recommends is not to be 'cramped and handicapped as a self-governing institution'. Suggestions indeed are made in the Report as to how dependence on central government grants could be drastically reduced by making fuel and motor taxes a local authority responsibility.

The result seems to satisfy Northern Ireland. A number of additional grants are paid by the Treasury, for example, to compensate for the effects on farming of distance from main markets, or to meet S.E.T. premium payments. The calculation of the quaintly named 'Imperial Contribution' gives a further advantage. This is the amount retained by Westminster to meet

Ulster's share of all United Kingdom services which it is either impossible or not customary to apportion on any geographical basis—defence, foreign affairs, agricultural subsidies, the funding of the national debt. The size of the retention is linked to the excess of revenue over necessary expenditure often setting off the additional cost of any services which are provided on a higher standard than in the rest of the country. The figure finally agreed by the joint Exchequer Board has been around £3·5m for some years, but in 1967–8 fell to the nominal sum of half a million.

There is plenty of room for argument as to what a 'fair' Imperial Contribution would be, but by any standards Northern Ireland is getting the services concerned at a bargain basement price. The evidence at least destroys the common view that separate control of internal finance would leave Scotland struggling on with the same handicaps as would arise from complete independence. So long as Scotland is part of the United Kingdom attention must be paid to the structural weaknesses of the economy north of the Border if only because it is in everyone's interest to have these eliminated. There is no need, however, to stick to the present system as though it and it alone can serve our purpose. The implication is almost that in some way the Scots escape by stealth with an unfair share of the booty.

Devolution is very different from separation in that it does not destroy the joint responsibility of the whole country for each and every part of it. What it might do, however, is to weaken Scotland's stake in central government and this is an important political, as distinct from financial, argument. If the number of Scots M.P.s was cut back, which might well be the consequence of a reform package which shifted a great deal of legislative business to Edinburgh, then the pressure on central government to remember specific Scottish interests could be reduced. Although as recently as 1955 the Tories had the largest single group of Scottish Members this could be particularly serious for a Labour administration which now tends to rely on a substantial majority in the north to give them a chance of survival in situations of near political balance. Such thoughts can concentrate the mind wonderfully when a decision has to be taken on, say, the need to maintain a strong Industrial Development Certificate policy.

The Irish are under-represented presumably because so much business is transacted in Stormont. It is difficult for them to make an impact because their group must be so small with only twelve seats to be contested. The Scots at least would always be at Westminster in significant numbers, although it is worth remembering that the average Northern Ireland electorate is over 76,000, or more than half as large again as that in Scotland. The Scottish proportion of one M.P. in eight is generous, certainly on a population basis, but it would be dangerously unfair to reduce Scotland's effective right to participate in decisions on defence or taxation. This risk might, however, be preferable to the logical alternative of keeping a full quota from north of the Border, but limiting their parliamentary activities to issues of common interest. This would raise sizable problems of demarcation and reduce the Scots for much of the time to the role of passive spectators. This may, of course, be unnecessary speculation. The creation of the G.L.C. did not lead to any reduction in the number of London M.P.s. That reorganization must, however, clearly be seen in the context of local government reform while what is now being suggested for Scotland is something much more fundamental.

If Scottish M.P.s were in effect excluded from a great deal of day-to-day parliamentary activity, Edinburgh could become for many politicians a more attractive prospect than London. A Scot in the United Kingdom cabinet might become a rarity—the Ulster Unionists have been conspicuously unsuccessful in this respect. Another casualty would almost inevitably be the office of Secretary of State, if only because the bulk of his responsibilities would be transferred to the Scottish Parliament and its ministers. The situation has greatly changed since June 1882 when Rosebery, responsible for Scottish affairs as an Under-Secretary at the Home Office, could write to Gladstone pointing out that 'from the day of the first meeting of the new parliament until the present day of its third session, if I am correctly informed, not one minute of Government time has been allotted to Scotland or Scottish affairs. Can you be surprised that the people of Scotland complain?' Today the Secretary of State holds a position of undoubted power, but equally of undoubted danger. No other political office is quite so exposed. The people still complain. Held responsible for every disappointment, Secretaries of State are remembered only for their failures. Tom Johnston probably alone left office with an enhanced reputation, but he operated during a party truce, resigning soon after the party war resumed with the coming of peace. Despite public scepticism the very presence of the Secretary of State adds greatly to the strength of the Scottish bargaining position. Legislation affecting Scotland will still be passed by the Westminster Parliament and the loss of a senior cabinet minister specifically charged with speaking on Scotland's behalf is not to be lightly discounted.

There are then disadvantages, and even in the financial field it is not clear that devolution would in itself lead to an increase in the resources available. There is an understandable unwillingness on the part of those involved to abandon a system which appears to produce satisfactory results. Anyone who considers that the fullest possible say in affairs at Westminster is the first priority must watch an experiment in devolution with anxiety. In spite of these doubts, the arguments for change are the more urgent. Widespread discontent will not fade away in the face of even the most determined efforts to pretend it does not exist. Government should be more open to influence, more accessible to those who will be affected by a particular decision. People suspect, and rightly suspect, that the Westminster machine needs not only an overhaul, but a reduced work load. To have legislators in London, administrators in Edinburgh, and a small corps of civil servants posting wildly between the two makes no sense. Dissatisfaction must not be allowed to drift into extremism. Even now it is all too easy to blame every difficulty on the indifference of Westminster. A Scottish Parliament would at least be responsible for its own mistakes and have to defend its own priorities. There could be no escape from that reality.

Recent governments have all supported the very great measure of administrative devolution which exists in Scotland. No doubt political pressures have contributed to this trend, but the developments have been hotly defended in terms of efficiency. Mr. Wilson's Cabinet has since 1966 moved further in the same direction, as can be seen from recent legislation affecting the transport and tourist industries. If there is a case for a system which administers Scottish affairs in a framework quite separate from that in existence south of the Border then many of the same arguments must point to an elected political counter-part. If the survival of unique institutions and, more importantly, of the traditions of independence has led to the Scottish Office as we know it, then the same differences and enthusiasms would do much to justify an Edinburgh Parliament to which St. Andrew's House could account for its actions. The patronage which goes with the right to make significant decisions would have an effect beyond the narrow field of politics. Edinburgh would be a more interesting place with more interesting people. A Parliament would do something to create the atmosphere and provide the audience and the money without which the arts must be inhibited. There is a real connection between political power and the survival of a culture.

The massive rebuff suffered by the S.N.P. in the municipal elections of May 1969 may alter some calculations. After a period of sensational success came reality; and their vote in the four cities dropped from around 180,000 in the previous year to just under 120,000. This may suggest the need for change is less urgent. But the case for devolution must be argued on its merits and it will be no disadvantage if discussion is not coloured by considerations of immediate electoral expediency. There is, however, clearly some evidence of hardening attitudes. Despite Quintin Hogg's stand, the Conservatives seem intent on ditching Edward Heath's so-called Declaration of Perth and the Home Committee considering how to give definition to the Leader of the Opposition's rather tentative gesture seems less and less likely to produce proposals which are both radical and acceptable to party activists.

Whatever the main parties may like to think, the Nationalists, on the evidence available, are at least going to be in a position to decide who wins seats even if they themselves cannot. The message here is an unhappy one for Labour. A third party is always likely to hit those in power and the S.N.P. have the ability, conspicuously lacking in the Liberals, to attract working-class support. This makes their emergence a particularly uncomfortable phenomenon. The first Nationalist success may well have been a reaction against unpopular economic measures, but at some point protest shades into commitment. It is far too early to write them off as a spent force quite incapable of influencing results at the next election. It would be a mistake to ignore the discontents on which they have been able to capitalize so effectively.

There is one feature common to almost all the opinion polls which could be of importance. Estimates have varied considerably as to the potential strength of the S.N.P., but the results have in almost every case revealed a gap between support for the party and for its policy. Mark Abrams puts the proportion of even Nationalist voters committed to separatism as low as 40 per cent (*Socialist Commentary*, February 1969) and this tends to confirm the findings of a Gallup poll which in September 1968 put popular approval at only 11 per cent. Work done by Strathclyde University in Glasgow (May 1968) and commissioned for the B.B.C. does nothing to alter this general picture. Equally clear, however, was the dissatisfaction with the *status quo*; the wish for change even if there was little agreement as to what form this should take. In these circumstances the sole achievement of those who argue that devolution is extravagant window-dressing likely to destroy administrative efficiency might well be to force moderates to vote for a party which does believe that problems will be solved if England becomes just another foreign country.

All this suggests that the politicians must be prepared to compete positively; for patient inaction is never an attractive programme. With the tide perhaps turning against the S.N.P. there is a temptation to suppress discussion about reform in case this is seen as weakness. An easing of the general economic position, the dissension and indeed tendency to fragment which almost always plagues a one-plank party faced with issues unconnected with its sole rallying cause, the inevitable concentration of publicity on the main challengers for power in general election conditions will all minimize the impact of nationalism. But this in itself will not be enough. What is also essential is a realistic approach which will attract the ordinary voter tempted to support the S.N.P. He must be reminded just how little he has in common with the hard-core separatist who looks forward to the day when Scotland sits in the United Nations between Saudi Arabia and Senegal.

The Labour Party in Scotland is still a long way from doing this. The situation has not been made any the easier by the certain knowledge that the Crowther Commission will not report before the 1970 election. The danger is that this will be seen as an effort to shelve the issue and that a genuine and constructive examination of a complex issue could in the public mind be swamped by the bitter controversies of Northern Ireland or the picturesque irrelevancies of the Manx constitution. In any event both Wheatley and Crowther must publish their findings. These, together with Maud, will have to be considered and reconciled. Vested interests must be consulted and where possible appeased before decisions can be taken. As a result Labour could face the electorate apparently as the party of the *status quo*, branded as conservative on what is clearly going to be a matter of concern to many. This might well be a tragedy, perhaps even a travesty, but it is not the less likely for that.

The Constitutional Commission will presumably take evidence before the end of this parliament. The Scottish Labour Party clearly cannot duck this and it is only to be hoped that a wish to avoid the appearance of giving ground to the Nationalists will not dictate too inflexible a stand. The statement accepted at the last party conference advanced the argument hardly at all. Home rule on the Northern Ireland pattern was rejected out-of-hand. The formula laid down—'the greatest possible devolution consistent with our absolute determination to retain the maximum possible influence on the economic and political policies of the United Kingdom'—was very little different from that adopted back in 1958. It is an acceptable sentiment which could offend no one. The difficulty is that ten years later the party is not one bit the nearer knowing what it means.

If, as suggested, the structure of government in Scotland remains an issue, it is not one which should be allowed to go by default. This matter should not be reduced to a narrow exercise in political tactics when what is required is anxious debate about the case for change. Constructive discussion could cut the ground from under the Nationalists whose success perhaps partly depends on being the only group now effectively campaigning on this point. This need not be the position. Labour has been traditionally sympathetic towards the arguments for devolution. James Barr's Home Rule Bill in 1927 was no isolated gesture and this very real interest was still a force in the early fifties. The present Government has been committed as no other to balanced industrial growth and the even spread of economic power. It would be in no way dishonourable or inconsistent for the Labour Party to think in terms of parallel political developments. I hope it is prepared to do so.

6

Federalism

DAVID STEEL

Federalism as a solution to the governmental relationships between the nations of the United Kingdom has a degree of historic respectability not often realized today. Much of the opposition to the Act of Union in 1707 stemmed from the belief in Scotland that if there had to be a Union it should not be an incorporating one in which the Scottish Parliament would disappear, but a federal one in which the Scots would retain their own internal government, which would have exclusive control over Scottish affairs and act as a lever in all dealings with England—if necessary as a lever to pull Scotland out of the Union should it be considered injurious to the interests of her people. As Professor Hanham has put it in his recent book: 'It is at least arguable that Texas got better terms when it joined the United States than Scotland got when it joined Great Britain.'[1]

When subsequent arguments raged over whether the Act of Union had been breached, they proved to be purely academic since there is no machinery for deciding whether a breach has occurred, still less any means of providing redress against such a breach. A federal constitution presupposes some written agreement between the parties entering the federation, any breach of which enables the federation to be dissolved. In the Act of Union all democratic and governmental machinery was removed from Scotland, leaving no means by which the process could be reversed. The Act stipulated that certain sections would apply 'for all time', but, as Sir Winston Churchill observed, the word 'never' is one which can only be used in general relativity to the subject. Equally, 'for all time' has since ceased to mean anything, since the Act of Union merely became a statute of the United Kingdom parliament

[1] H. J. Hanham, *Scottish Nationalism*, London, 1969, p. 66.

which is itself sovereign and therefore free to ignore or repeal such statutes or parts of statutes as it pleases.

In the latter half of the nineteenth century the Scottish Home Rule Association seems largely to have consisted of people anxious to restore to a Scottish Parliament full control over Scottish affairs without breaking up the United Kingdom. Following Gladstone's espousal of Home Rule for Ireland and after the 1886 general election, he published a pamphlet largely on the future of Ireland which drew attention to the need to reform the whole of government in Britain in a manner more consistent with the aspirations of the individual nations within it. It is from this time that the Liberal Party's commitment to federalism can be traced. In 1888 the annual conference of the Scottish Liberal Association passed a resolution calling for the granting of 'Home Rule legislatures on a Federal basis to Scotland, England, Ireland and Wales'. Similar resolutions have ever since been passed with monotonous regularity at almost every annual conference of the Scottish Liberal Association (since 1945, the Scottish Liberal Party), the latest one being in 1969.

The Scottish Home Rule Association embraced many Liberals, some Tories, and a considerable number of Socialists. Keir Hardie was one of its vice-presidents and Ramsay MacDonald secretary of its London branch, and its emphasis was on a federal solution. Prime Minister Asquith committed the Liberal Government to 'Home Rule All Round' in 1912 as soon as the Irish Bill could be got out of the way first. In 1913 a 'Government of Scotland' Bill was introduced and approved by the House of Commons. It was designed to give Scotland an internal parliament, but was thwarted by the Tory majority in the House of Lords until the outbreak of the First World War the following year. In 1919 the Commons carried a resolution calling for a committee to introduce a federal constitution for Britain, and a Speaker's Conference was duly appointed. It failed to produce any satisfactory solution. In the same year, the Labour Party's Scottish Council called for the establishment of a Scottish parliament with full control over domestic affairs, leaving defence, colonial and foreign affairs to Westminster. Likewise did the Scottish T.U.C.

Even the founding of the Scottish National Party in 1934[1]

[1] By the amalgamation of the National Party of Scotland, founded in 1928 and the Scottish Party, founded in 1932.

presupposed, although it did not use the words, some form of federal constitution. Its policy statement referred to the creation in Scotland of 'a Parliament which shall be the *final authority on all Scottish affairs* including taxation and finance' (my italics). Scotland and England were to 'set up machinery to deal jointly with' the empire, defence, foreign policy, and customs—in other words much the same division of responsibilities as advocated by federalists today. The development of the separatist viewpoint is therefore comparatively recent, and can be said to stem largely from the new aims and objects of the S.N.P. adopted in 1946 demanding a totally sovereign parliament merely seeking to co-operate with England in whatever fields it could.

The federalists (i.e. mainly the Liberal Party, though recently this policy has been adopted officially by *The Scotsman* newspaper) have continued to advocate what is therefore historically the principal basis of the case for Scottish Home Rule. In 1962 the Scottish Liberal Party published its up-to-date view in *Scottish Self Government*, which did not specifically stress federalism but called for a domestic Scottish parliament and a joint Exchequer Board operating between England and Scotland. In 1966 the Liberal M.P.s revived the historic practice of introducing self-government Bills in the Commons. Russell Johnston, M.P. for Inverness, sponsored one which was given an unopposed formal first reading under the ten-minute rule, but which was never given time for a full second-reading debate. In February 1968 the Liberal leader, Jeremy Thorpe, introduced a Federal Government Bill under the same procedure and with the same results, thus up-dating the 'Home Rule All Round' policy of his predecessors.

I have tried before to define the aims of the federalists as 'the maximum amount of home rule consistent with common sense'. The philosophy behind it is really an extension of Abraham Lincoln's classic definition of democratic government—'government of the people, by the people and for the people'—to government 'near the people' as well. It is commonly accepted that as government becomes year by year more complicated and increasingly impinges on the daily life of the citizen, so it becomes more necessary to decentralize power.

In a pamphlet published in 1968, *Out of Control—a critical examination of the Government of Scotland*, I argued that this general proposition was particularly true of Scotland and that the various well-meaning steps taken over the years to transfer more of Scotland's administration from London ministries to the Scottish Office had resulted in a serious imbalance between the executive and democratic parliamentary control. The immense range of ministerial responsibilities which rests in the hands of the Secretary of State for Scotland results in practice in the greater concentration of power in the hands of the civil servants, while the minister's functions are themselves less open to parliamentary scrutiny than those of his several English counterparts. One of my minor recommendations to correct this has since been put into effect—the setting up of a House of Commons Select Committee on Scottish Affairs. The fundamental weakness remains unchanged: administrative and executive power over many fields exists in Scotland without the necessary corresponding legislative and parliamentary machinery. The present government of Scotland is largely irresponsible in the proper sense of the word.

All of this could lead equally to the conclusion that Scotland should be a separate sovereign state just as much as a federal one, but federalists differ from the separatists on two basic counts. There is first the economic argument.

As Dr. Gavin McCrone has carefully argued in a chapter on the consequences of separation in his recent book[1] a market of five millions is too small for a large part of modern industry and it would therefore be essential to safeguard duty-free access for Scottish goods to the English market. Much of the major industrial investment in Scotland of the past decade (certainly the American part) has taken place with a view to access to a European market and in anticipation of a possible entry by Britain into the Common Market. If Scottish manufactured goods had to surmount tariff walls to get even into England, industrial investment would certainly be frightened off.

The separatists argue that a sovereign Scotland would not wish to create tariff barriers for this very reason, in which case Scotland would not be able to prevent a free flow of English goods into Scotland. They believe that Scotland should establish a customs and tariffs union with England. Since England is overwhelmingly the more powerful economic unit, this would mean in effect accepting such an arrangement dictated on English terms. There

[1] *Scotland's Future: The Economics of Nationalism*, Oxford, 1969.

would be no reason for England to be altruistic and damage her own interests to benefit an independent Scotland.

With a separate Scotland, we should cease automatically to gain from all the directional controls established over the development of industry, such as the refusal of industrial development certificates. A sovereign England with its own separate parliament would only be interested in measures to improve the economic and social well-being of its English citizens and not of the neighbouring Scottish foreigners. With a federal parliament, no question of tariff barriers would arise and the political party in power in it would be subject to the normal political and electoral pressures from each of the component states to ensure economic fair play.

The second and more fundamental disagreement between the separatists and the federalists rests on a totally different view of the role of the nation state. Liberals are primarily internationalist in outlook, which means that we accept as both inevitable and desirable the diminution in importance of the sovereign nation in favour of a more ordered international scene. This is true in the field of defence. It is in our view hopelessly unrealistic for Scotland to consider that she could be in any meaningful sense defended independently of her neighbours. Indeed, we believe that the concept of *Britain* being independent in defence is itself only a dangerous illusion. As mankind becomes more civilized we extend the definition of 'neighbour' from family to tribe, from tribe to region, from region to nation, and from nation to the international community. The development of modern weapons of war of terrifying scale has accelerated this process. No nation is an island entire of itself. Most nations now accept this fact and surrender part of their own sovereignty to some international body such as N.A.T.O. in return for greater security.

In the economic field, too, we believe that some surrender of national sovereignty can be of mutual benefit. It is no coincidence that the Liberal Party stood alone in advocating in 1956 that Britain should be a founder-member of the European Economic Community and help to shape it. We saw the Common Market developing not only as an economic unit but also as a political one, eventually forming a united federal Europe. The logic of our case is that ideally Scotland should be a federal state not in a Great Britain federation but in a European federation, and that still remains our long-term objective. Looking even further ahead we hope that one day the United Nations Organization will prove to be merely the ill-developed embryo of a world government. Only when the individual nations of the world are prepared to surrender sufficient sovereignty to an international democratic authority will there be any guarantee of a lasting peace and a greater distribution of wealth among mankind.

I have found when addressing Nationalist meetings both in my own constituency and in London that such views as I have just outlined are met with a mixture of dismay and horror. Therefore, united as we are in our determination to establish a Scottish Parliament and regain control over our own affairs, and though agreed on the beneficial effect a focus of political power in Scotland would have on the social, cultural, and economic life of our country, there remains a deep and fundamental division in philosophy between federalism and nationalism.

It is, moreover, worth asking whether for Scotland—small and attached as she is physically to a larger neighbour—the concept of total sovereignty has any real meaning. Our neighbours of similar size on either side of us, Denmark and Eire, have found their freedom of movement severely restricted. Eire devalued within minutes of Britain. Both have applied to join the E.E.C., withdrawn their applications, and then reapplied at precisely the same time as the United Kingdom Government. In theory they are sovereign states free to do as they please; in practice their sovereignty is limited by the facts of life. Hence talk by the S.N.P. about how Scotland ought to be free to decide separately from England whether or not to go into Europe is both excellent in principle and utterly meaningless. Nor do federalists share the S.N.P. enthusiasm for the panoply of Scottish embassies round the world.

The greatest difficulty facing the federalists, however, is the fact that federalism is a complicated policy. The S.N.P. have the advantage of a simplistic (one might say naïve) approach to the electorate which is easily put across. Federalism is not only difficult to expound, it has never in fact been outlined in precise detail for Britain. It is easier to begin by setting down what it does not mean rather than what it does mean. It does not mean an 'Ulster' or 'Stormont' solution for Scotland. To grant Scotland a parliament while Westminster continued to be at one and the same time the English and the U.K. Parliament would be profoundly unsatisfactory. This is not to deny the limited success of Stormont, for example, in creating new jobs and in creating a powerful focus of political life, but Ulster's representation at Westminster is limited to twelve Members, and they carry very little weight, the best political talent going to Stormont. Indeed, their ability to vote and speak on purely English or Scottish domestic matters is resented and is anomalous while Westminster cannot interfere in Ulster's domestic policies.

Nor does federalism mean that Scotland would merely, together with the regions of England, have a provincial council possibly with a grander name. This is the solution logically and carefully advocated by the Labour M.P., John Mackintosh, in his book *The Devolution of Power*.[1] This is regionalism. There is no suggestion, for example, that each of the regions should have a separate criminal law, yet Scotland has retained her own legal system and should be fully free to develop it. There is every case for establishing regional councils in England, but this is a distinct and separate question from the case for Scottish (and therefore English) home rule.

Federalism was practised by some of the city states of Ancient Greece and in the Middle Ages by some of the Italian cities. Its longest running present-day practitioner is Switzerland, which traces its development from the banding together of three cantons in 1291. A loose federation is usually called a confederation and therefore constitutional purists use the two words distinctly to describe the basic division between the two standard forms of federal constitution. Unfortunately, as there is no clearly established usage here, I must state the distinction I propose to make. A 'federation' is a grouping of states in which the powers of the individual states are precisely defined with the undefined 'reserve of powers' going to the central federal government. The object of precisely defining powers is to limit that power. Hence, in a 'federation' such as Canada, the central government is extremely strong, while the powers of the provinces are strictly defined. A 'confederation' is a grouping of states in which the powers of the central government are carefully defined and the reserve of powers rest with the individual states. In this way a strict check is kept on the authority of the central government, as in Australia.

[1] London, 1968

Many modern nations such as America, West Germany, Yugoslavia, and Switzerland operate variations on these two themes. The federalists in Scotland lean towards a 'confederal' solution in which powers, for example, of taxation would rest primarily with the individual states. The written division of powers means that both the legislature of the federation and that of each of the federating units are limited in their scope and neither of these is supreme. A federal court is usually established to settle any disputes between the two.

A particular difficulty arises in creating a federal structure within Britain: namely, that the population of England is greater than those of Scotland, Wales, and Ireland put together. The other three states would not wish to be dictated to by a purely English majority, nor would the English majority wish to be under the thumbs of the collective minority of the other three states. The most frequently advocated solution to this dilemma is the continuance of a two-chamber federal parliament, the lower chamber elected on a popular basis throughout the U.K. and the upper chamber representing equally or near equally the four nation states. Another solution would be to have only a unicameral federal legislature with weighted voting of the kind familiar in the institutions of the E.E.C. to protect the interests of the smaller states. There tends to be an over-obsession with this question of voting. In practice in existing federations the states do not gang up against each other—the federal parliaments tend to divide on party lines and not on state lines.

In a speech in May 1969 Mr. Jo Grimond, the former Liberal leader, developed the prospect of learning from the E.E.C. a stage further:

> In my view it is clear that we need to look at the Community idea as developed in the E.E.C. and adapt it to our needs. The Communities have major faults. They are becoming somewhat bureaucratic. They lack a democratic element. But they deal with the sort of problems we shall have to deal with and they have shown that new political concepts will work. I see therefore not a full federal parliament but a commission or commissions meeting to thrash out particular economic and political problems where harmonization is important. Their directive would come from the initial constitutional treaty—as the Commissions in Brussels look to the Treaty of Rome. They should, I believe, be small. Their composition is a matter for

discussion, but I see them either composed of ministers of the constituent countries, with a small permanent staff, or with a limited number of representatives from the parliaments of each country. Their decisions would need ratification, I would imagine, and would be implemented by the civil service of each country.

I find this idea more attractive than saddling ourselves with all the weight of conventional nineteenth-century federal apparatus. There is plenty of room for debate of this kind to continue among federalists.

Finally, it is worth stressing that opinion polls have shown consistently in Scotland that it is the federal rather than separatist approach which is desired by most Scots—even by those who support the S.N.P. It is also the basis of the policy adopted by the General Assembly of the Church of Scotland, although they do not use the word federal and rightly stress the desire to 'enable the people of Scotland to choose the form of self-government best suited to the nation's well-being'. James Davidson, Liberal M.P. for West Aberdeenshire, has in this Parliament introduced a Referendum Bill enabling the Scots to do just that, but it was heavily outvoted by the united might of the Labour and Conservative Parties.

The two home-rule parties in Scotland—the Liberals and the Nationalists—could effectively campaign together on this theme of the Scots having the right to decide the future for themselves (including the right to total sovereignty and separation if so desired). This possibility has been so far rejected by the S.N.P., who insist that all should adopt their own doctrines. Thus the granting of any Scottish parliament may be long delayed. For the British Government the lesson of Ireland should serve as a warning. The Conservative Party obstructed Irish demands for internal home rule and Gladstone's plans for a federal kingdom were never implemented. Accordingly, the Irish demanded total independence. The result has been the disunity of these islands and the comparative impoverishment of many of the people of Eire. Federalists believe that it would be a tragedy if the same mistakes were to be repeated in Scotland.

7

The Case for Independence

IAIN S. M. MacCORMICK

The case for independence is concerned with control over the internal and the external affairs of Scotland. In a world of nation states it seems right that, if Scotland is a nation, the Scottish people should control their own domestic affairs, and make their own distinctive contribution on the international scene. Because they believe that Scotland is a nation, the fundamental aim of Scottish nationalists is independence for Scotland. Moreover, they believe that the country is in present circumstances misgoverned and bled of initiative through the lack of self-government. These beliefs are the main subject matter of this essay.

It is worth considering first, and necessarily in general terms, the extent to which the people of Scotland desire to assert themselves as a nation. However well or ill the case for independence is made out in this essay, the matter will eventually be settled in practice by the people of Scotland as arbiters of their country's destiny. There can be little argument but that in the last few years the political climate in Scotland has undergone a profound change, to the extent that the next general election will be fought, in Scotland, around the issue of self-government for Scotland. The present activities of all the political parties are a guarantee of this, as will be seen. Outside Scotland, the majority of political commentators seems credulously to assume that this situation represents a quite new phenomenon in the political life of the country. The recent electoral successes of the Scottish National Party are a novelty. But their foundation has been a process of political re-education which has developed, in organized form, over the last forty or so years; the origins of which are to be seen in the nineteenth century in a recognizably modern form.

The nineteenth-century forerunners of today's Scottish

nationalists were mainly Liberals whose national aspirations were awakened or encouraged by the controversy over the question of Irish Home Rule. Such people anticipated the resentment felt by many Scots in 1953 when the present monarch assumed the title 'Elizabeth II', by raising sustained and organized protest at the historical insult and absurdity inherent in the description of Queen Victoria's successor as Edward VII of Great Britain (and hence, by implication, of Scotland also).

In 1928 the National Party of Scotland was founded, largely at the instigation of a small group of Glasgow University students led by John M. MacCormick. This move enabled the proponents of self-government to coalesce, and infused a moribund movement with new life and the prospects of activity, because it was the aim of the National Party to work for a change in Scotland's status constitutionally, by contesting parliamentary elections. Until the outbreak of the Second World War, the National Party was able to make a considerable impact politically.[1] The movement of which it was the core also produced a national reawakening in a cultural and literary sense, although I regret that I cannot adequately assess this here.

During the war, and in the 1950s, the National Party ceased to be the main focus of anti-Union activity in Scotland. And in the late 1940s and early 1950s the initiative passed to the more broadly based Scottish Covenant Association, which was, again, the inspiration of John M. MacCormick, whose election in 1950 as Lord Rector of Glasgow University was an indication of the strength of popular feeling at that time. The Scottish Covenant Association amassed some two million signatures from the adult population of Scotland for the Scottish Covenant which proclaimed a programme of constitutional change for Scotland not unlike that of the Liberal Party today. The Covenant brought the issue of home rule before the people of Scotland more strikingly than ever before. It did so, however, at the expense of being a vehicle of immediate change, since its broad base was achieved by its policy of not contesting parliamentary seats. Thus has the process of the political reawakening of the people of Scotland proceeded virtually without break, albeit with changing emphasis, and often through agencies whose programmes for the future of

---

[1] Particularly after the fusion with the Scottish Party in 1934 to form the Scottish National Party, which name has not changed since then.

Scotland were less ambitious than that of the Scottish National Party today.

Today, the only force in politics which can conceivably achieve any degree of self-government for Scotland is the Scottish National Party, the stated aim of which is the establishment of Scotland as a sovereign state. The extent to which other organizations now endorse, or pretend to endorse, programmes or proposals for legislative devolution for Scotland is a measure of the feeling of the Scots people on the issue, since it reflects a desire to win votes and support which would otherwise go to the Scottish National Party. This reflection applies in varying degrees to both the Labour Party and the Conservative Party. It applies to the Scottish Trades Union Congress and to the Communist Party. The Liberal Party has consistently supported the setting up of federal government in Britain, which proposal is now the main plank of its platform in Scotland. The Liberal Party's programme for Scottish home rule has in the 1960s proved a great vote-winner in Scotland; as witness the fact that five of the Liberal M.P.s sit for Scottish constituencies. Much, however, of the support which the Liberals received in the 1966 election presumably emanated from Nationalists who either had no S.N.P. candidate for whom to vote, or who regarded the Liberal Party as the only credible political force aligned in roughly the right direction. The recent growth, and success, of the Scottish National Party has changed all that.

The Labour Party's attitude to a meaningful degree of legislative devolution in Scotland is a comment on that party's desertion of its radical origins. Before, and during, the Second World War the Labour Party supported home rule for Scotland. But after Labour's runaway victory at the end of the war, the matter was quietly dropped, probably for no better reason than that in party political terms Labour needs the Scottish vote. The ageing placemen who make up a majority of the Scottish Labour M.P.s are the natural product of the stultifying of a once genuinely radical and Scottish movement. The two-party system acts, and is bound to act, so as to cut across the interests of Scotland and to substitute the political squabbling between right and left, which is the chief *raison d'être* of the English-based parties.

Whatever Harold Wilson may say, it is the Conservative Party which is in British politics the party of pragmatism, and to some

D

extent this has been reflected in that party's dealings with Scotland. The Conservatives can, for example, justly boast that compared with the Labour Party they have been the pacemakers in advancing administrative devolution in Scotland. That apart, however, the whole ethos of the Scottish Conservative and Unionist Party must make it in the long run the chief political obstacle to the realization of nationalist aspirations. Perhaps such a role is implicit in the very name of the party; but there is more to it than that. For even now the Scottish Conservatives receive their inspiration chiefly from the monied and/or landed aristocracy; from the only section of Scottish society which it is difficult to differentiate from its English counterpart. Educated in England, living between London and their Scottish estates, entrenched as part of the British Establishment, such 'upper-class' Scots represent a superb example of racial integration. And it is scarcely surprising that most such people are unable to discern those elements in the Scottish situation which have prompted so many others to campaign for Scotland's independence.

More consideration will be given later to the present attitudes of the Labour and Conservative Parties towards Scottish Home Rule. Suffice it to say for the moment that the S.N.P. has already clearly been able to jump the 'credibility gap' across which the unionist parties have previously been able to isolate themselves, scarcely deigning to discuss the issue of self-government at all.

It is not my aim to draw a parallel between nationalism in Scotland and nationalism elsewhere. It would nonetheless be foolish to proceed in the pretence that now, of all times, such a movement can exist in a vacuum, uninfluenced by events in other countries. Our opponents often make the mistake of describing Scottish nationalism as a parochial anachronism in an age of internationalism. Yet it is a matter of observation and not one of debate that the period which has elapsed since the Second World War has seen the emergence of more independent countries than has any other similar period of modern history. Internationalism today denotes no more than the willingness of sovereign states to participate in attempts to bring order to the world through such associations as the United Nations; or the desire to make arrangements of mutual convenience, such as those enshrined in the Treaty of Rome. And, as always, states agree to co-operate in the interests of their common defence.

Nevertheless, there are those who claim that, in terms of international relations, Scotland's present absorption in the Union with England affords a selfless example which might with benefit be imitated by other countries. This kind of apologetic for Scotland's present position is typical of an attitude in Scots dubbed by the late Professor Ian Henderson the 'disloyalty syndrome'. It gives rise to a wide variety of absurdities. For example, the present Secretary of State for Scotland has gone to the grotesque length of defending the fact that in certain universities in Scotland nearly half the students are from England, by claiming this as a great contribution to internationalism in education. But internationalism must involve reciprocity in such matters; and in no English university is there more than a tiny percentage of Scots students. Indeed, it is the common denominator of all arguments of that type that the things which are said to be good for Scotland are certainly not widely regarded as being good for England. Whoever has heard an Englishman exclaim with pride that in 1707 his country gave up her sovereignity in search of a higher ideal?

Nationalism in Scotland today is essentially practical—'patriotism at work' as *The Scotsman* recently described it—but it depends also on the concept of Scotland as a nation. And however much the essential distinctions between Scotland and England may have become blurred over the centuries, the number of Scots who regard their country as a nation and who wish to reassert its rights as such is certainly increasing. Historically, Scotland is one of the oldest nations in Europe with a distinct tradition of culture and civilization long more widely recognized and appreciated in continental Europe than in England. The ancient Kingdom of Scotland was in no sense a left-over from the Anglo-Saxon Heptarchy. It was politically independent of, and most of the Scots were ethnically distinct from, their southern neighbours. From the eleventh century, however, Scotland began to adopt institutions similar to those of England; notably a dialect of Anglo-Saxon, and a feudal aristocracy. But despite such developments, Scotland maintained her national character throughout the Middle Ages. And the same was true, with short intermissions, of Scotland's political independence, although it was continually at peril because of the aggressive propensities of successive English kings who regarded Scotland, as they regarded Wales and Ireland, as a legitimate area for territorial aggrandisement.

In 1603, King James VI succeeded to the throne of England. In an age of royal absolutism, it was he who established the principle that Scotland was best ruled, by pen, from London. The Scottish monarchy became effectively English. In the long run the consequent disregard of Scottish interests on the part of the executive arm of government could only produce one of two results: separation again, or complete political union. Not least in the interests of their own national security, the English, aided by a group of Scottish aristocrats, set about securing the Treaty of Union which was concluded in 1707.

In theory, the parliaments of both Scotland and England agreed to suppress the separate sovereignties of their respective nations, and to co-operate in the establishment of a new nation, the United Kingdom. In his book, *The Devolution of Power*, J. P. Mackintosh, M.P. writes (of Scotland) '. . . the country was not incorporated into England, but accepted a Treaty of Union in 1707'.[1] But what happened was not as straightforward and equitable as Mackintosh implies. By the letter of the law, Scotland may not have been incorporated in England. By the letter of the law, certain Scottish institutions were specifically protected against future interference or absorption. In practice, on the other hand, the main institution through which Scotland's nationhood could be given practical expression *was* absorbed without trace into its English counterpart. For such was the fate of the Scottish Parliament. All the constitutional evidence available goes to show that the present British Parliament is none other than the old English Parliament continuing. All that happened, following upon the Treaty of Union, was the admission of a disproportionately low number of Scottish members to the House of Commons, and of Scottish peers to the House of Lords. As if to illustrate this point, the 'British' Parliament celebrated its seven hundredth anniversary in 1965.

The Scottish legislature was thus abolished, but the Treaty of Union guaranteed also the continuance of three other important Scottish institutions: the Church of Scotland, the Scots legal system, and the Scots mint. The mint did not survive the Treaty for long. The two former have, however, maintained their independence although both have from time to time been shown vulnerable in the face of the theory, and practice, of English parliamentary sovereignty; a theory which reduces observance of

[1] J. P. Mackintosh, *The Devolution of Power*, London, 1968, p. 150.

the terms of the Treaty of Union to the level either of a gentlemen's agreement or of a matter of expediency.

Of late, the fashion has grown of describing Scotland as one of the various 'regions' of Britain. The existence of two such ancient and noble institutions as the Kirk and the Scots legal system is a welcome obstacle to such slovenly thinking, since the only sense in which Scotland can be described as a region is the geographical sense. The Church in particular provides a focus of national consciousness; especially as its General Assembly provides a national forum for debate ranging over all Scotland's affairs.

Historically, then, Scotland is a nation; even today retaining some of the attributes of nationhood and a distinct identity. It is, nevertheless, also true that the march of time will see an intensification of the similarities which already exist between Scottish and English attitudes, ways of life, and national institutions. The process of assimilation continues, jogged along by the influence of mass media. At the same time, however, the strength of political Scottish nationalism has in recent times increased, because, as has already been indicated, the case of modern Scottish nationalism is practical rather than theoretical. It derives more from a study of the disadvantages with which the present system of government has saddled the people of Scotland, than from pure contemplation of the abstraction which is Scotland's history and tradition.

It is arguable that in the short term the Treaty of Union was of help to Scotland in that it removed barriers to trade which would probably have obstructed the development of the Industrial Revolution. But in the eighteenth and nineteenth centuries the responsibilities of the government were so circumscribed (by modern standards) as to preclude all but the most tentative interference by government in the business affairs of the country. Thus the Industrial Revolution in Scotland was directed by Scottish businessmen and encouraged by Scottish investment. As the responsibilities of government enlarged and as its powers of interference and supervision grew, so did the harmful long term effects of Union become progressively more apparent; since, vis-à-vis the Scottish economy, indeed Scottish life in general, the new powers of government were exercised from far away and were used to formulate policies primarily for another country with different problems. The case for independence centres round the necessity, under modern conditions, of transferring the centre of political power and decision-making to Scotland: this in the interests, first, of better government for the people of Scotland; second, of Scotland taking her rightful place amongst the nations of the world.

In his book *The Claim of Scotland*, H. J. Paton makes the point that for a period ending in the First World War Scotland was one of the richest countries in the world, perhaps even richer in terms of her population than was England in relation to hers. Such was the situation when, compared with today at least, the philosophy of *laissez faire* was rampant with regard to government, and before the theory of economies of scale had demanded the wholesale take-over of Scottish enterprises by concerns south of the Border. Now, however, the situation has changed entirely. Far from being a vigorous centre of industrial and financial enterprise, very nearly the whole of Scotland now constitutes what is euphemistically termed a 'development area'. The influence of the government extends into every corner of the economy. Many former independent business concerns have become branches of English firms. Both of these processes are the inevitable concomitants of life in a modern state, but they need not be the cause of the worst housing problem, and the worst emigration problem, of any country in Western Europe.

We are accused of being behind the times; we are told that it is old-fashioned to think in terms of national sovereignties. Yet it is precisely because our present system of government does not and cannot meet up to the demands of modern conditions that we seek independence. This increasing complexity of modern government, as applied in Scotland, has been palliated by successive Westminster governments by the introduction of various measures of administrative devolution of a nature which recognizes the special status of Scotland as opposed to the regions of England. The office of Secretary for Scotland was created in 1885. And at present the Secretary of State, assisted by a Minister of State and three Under-Secretaries, presides over four Scottish Civil Service departments. These are the Scottish Home and Health Department, the Scottish Agriculture and Fisheries Department, the Scottish Education Department, and the Scottish Development Department. The Secretary of State is thus responsible for the administration in Scotland of a very wide range of the activities of government, although there are also areas under the direct control of English ministries—notably the Ministry of Transport, the Board of Trade, the Ministry of Fuel and Power, the Ministry of Technology, and the Department of Employment and Productivity.

One of the more facile jibes of the opponents of the case for independence is that, in view of the extent of administrative devolution in Scotland, many of the important decisions in Scottish affairs are already taken in Scotland. Hence, the argument can be extended, there is no need for any kind of self-government for Scotland; and the present system benefits Scotland by entitling her to an annual hand-out of largesse from England, and to her place in the queue of 'regions' clamouring to the Board of Trade for industry to be directed in the right direction. (Thus far, and significantly, in view of the passions already aroused by this whole question, the Government has issued no set of figures comprehensive enough to allow of the calculation of Scotland's present solvency, or to allow of proof of the inherently unlikely proposition that Scotland is actually, or potentially, unable to match the rich small states of Europe.)

The weakness of the argument lies in the nature of the decisions made by the Secretary of State for Scotland. Obviously, such decisions cannot be of principle. Decisions of principle are made by the government and enacted by parliament, and the Secretary of State's function is to make the relatively minor decisions which transform government policy into action. Nationalists in Scotland sometimes make the mistake of portraying the Secretary of State as an unrepresentative Prime Minister of Scotland, with responsibility as well for the administration of too many aspects of government. It might be better if he were, for the truth regrettably is that the Prime Minister of Britain is Scotland's Prime Minister, and the Secretary of State is his representative in Scotland. He is a member of the Cabinet and shares responsibility for its decisions, almost all of which are made to suit English conditions.

Even in the area where discretion is left to the Scottish Office, in practice the decisions made tend to correspond very closely with those made by English Departments for England. J. P. Mackintosh puts it succinctly: 'The great pride of the civil service is not that it has developed special methods or a different emphasis in Scotland, but rather that no gap can be found between Edinburgh and London methods. . . .'[1] The futility of imagining that

---

[1] op. cit., p. 132.

the sort of administrative devolution which has been landed on Scotland can do anything other than pass on the decisions of central government is perhaps well illustrated by pointing out that in an independent Scotland a civil service similar to the present one will exist; but it will then exist to administer decisions made by a Scottish government, and tailored to suit Scottish needs. In the wider question of how well or how badly Scotland is governed, the degree of administrative devolution Scotland has is totally irrelevant.

In terms of population, Scotland is only a fraction of the size of England. This single fact does much to explain the unsatisfactory relationship between the two countries under the present system of government. Geographically, it is all too easy for an establishment which thinks in terms of the north of England as being remote, to consider Scotland as an even more peripheral extension. Politically, the hard facts of democracy demand that government's chief preoccupations must be with the deep south where the majority of the population live, and where the maximum number of votes is to be garnered. It is therefore a feature of the present system of government that no real attempt is made to differentiate between the effect of legislation in the area for which it was primarily formulated and its effect in Scotland where conditions are often dramatically different.

That is the crux of the matter, for those who oppose the aims of the nationalists are, at least by default, conniving at a situation wherein it will no longer be possible to consider Scotland as a social and economic entity at all. As time passes this process accelerates, and its effects will spread to every aspect of the life of Scotland. Anyone who doubts the reality of this process, or the deadly dangers to Scottish life inherent in it, would be well advised to read the recent report of the Scottish Council for Development and Industry entitled *Centralization*. Therein, the debilitating effects of the constant removal of decision-making in business to points south of the Border are discussed. And the report is not thinking in terms of a point of no return somewhere in the unforeseeable future; it locates it somewhere in the next two or three decades. Sometimes, the move of the decision-making has been the direct result of legislation—for instance, in the case of those nationalized concerns in Scotland where control is exercised from England. More usually, however, the trend is simply the result of there being no Scottish agency which can supervise such moves in the best interests of the people of Scotland. As has already been indicated, the situation is constantly exacerbated by legislation of a general nature which is harmful in Scotland. While it is not my place to discuss the economic case for independence, I would mention here the unfortunate effects in Scotland of the deflationary measures known as the 'Freeze'—measures inevitably applied to Scotland but designed to combat an inflationary situation existing in England; to say even less about the ridiculous impost Selective Employment Tax, and the crippling burden being placed on the Scotch whisky industry by penal rates of duty.

While it may satisfy some to see Scotland as a branch of England, and Scottish industry relegated to branch factory status, the dangers are obvious. Such industry is especially vulnerable in times of recession; such an emasculated economic life will be accompanied by further emigration and a consequent imbalance in the composition of society. It is simply not credible that such a deep-seated defect in the present system can be rectified by anything other than drastic change: change which will give Scotland a legislature of her own and the powers to frame laws pertinent to the Scottish situation; change, which of itself, by situating in Scotland a focus of decision and a centre of government, will tend to act as a magnet for economic activity. And without changing the ownership of any firms who have been the object of successful take-overs, a Scottish Government will be able to act so as to ensure that the activities of all business concerns are in accordance with Scotland's interests.

It is obvious also that such major changes internally will have to be accompanied by changes in Scotland's relationships with other countries, particularly England. Or, to be more accurate, Scotland must be able to create relationships with other countries, and to arrive at a more meaningful relationship with England than the present one. At present, Scotland's representatives in the Commons are in a permanent minority of eight to one. Even if a majority of, or even all, the Scottish M.P.s supported a motion calling for Scottish independence (or, of course, anything else) the English majority would be quite within their constitutional rights to vote against it. In the case of eleven Home Rule Bills in the past this has actually happened. Not, of course, that the M.P.s who represent constituencies in Scotland act for Scotland as such, except perhaps incidentally in the course of pressing the interests of their own constituencies. The framework of government and the development of the two-party system combine to ensure that the 'Scottish' M.P.s are reft between the two main parties and that consequently Scottish affairs have no united mouthpiece in parliament.

In terms of Scotland's relations with countries outside the British Isles, play is often made by unionists of left and right with the notion that an independent Scotland would be an isolated Scotland, starved of foreign investment and shunned by foreign diplomats. Here I would emphasize again the outward-looking aspect of Scottish Nationalism. It is precisely because so many Scots now feel that they have a positive contribution to make to European and world affairs, that to them independence is such an attractive option. At present, simply, Scotland as such is effectively isolated from meaningful contacts with other countries. In the future, Scotland must have such contacts, not only to make her distinctive contribution on the international scene, but also as an essential extension of the life of the economy.

From various quarters, palliatives which fall short of independence are being offered to the people of Scotland. These range from further administrative devolution to the federalism proposed by the Liberal Party. Neither the Labour Party nor the Conservative Party favours any kind of legislative devolution, although they have reacted to the recent upsurge of nationalism by being seen to toy with the idea. The Labour Government has set up a Royal Commission under Lord Crowther; the Conservatives a Constitution Committee under Sir Alec Douglas-Home. The position of both parties was neatly paraphrased in a recent statement by the Council of the Scottish Labour Party: 'We wish to obtain the greatest possible devolution consistent with our absolute determination to retain the maximum possible influence on the economic and political policies of the United Kingdom.' Well, the 'maximum possible influence on the economic and political policies of the United Kingdom' has so far produced a peculiarly poor return for Scotland. And one of the main reasons, as has been seen, is precisely that it precludes meaningful devolution. Anyway, it is more probable than not that the Labour Party and the Tory Party are in their eyes weathering a temporary nationalist storm by holding out the hope that they are genuinely interested in legislative devolution. Further administrative devolution, an increase perhaps in the number of *ad hoc* Boards and Commissions: neither will change the character of government in Scotland nor associate the people more closely with the important decisions of government.

Regional solutions to the problem have been suggested, notably by J. P. Mackintosh M.P. But while they would increase the democratic aspect of government in regional affairs (Scotland would count as a region), the regional parliaments would exercise only a strictly designated range of powers, and the central government in London would remain firmly in control of all the major policy decisions. Scotland, as one of eleven regions, would still suffer from policies framed with the south in mind. Scotland would remain isolated from the affairs of the world. Scotland's position would fall far short of nationhood.

The Liberals' idea of a federal system of government for Britain comes much closer to the nationalist aim of independence. Again, however, this would involve the retention by the Westminster Government of a list of powers which would certainly include, for example, the conduct of foreign affairs and defence, and might also include the levying of taxes and duties. Because of the disparity of size between Scotland and England, problems would be sure to arise in the federal parliament where Scotland's representation would be likely to be in the same proportion as at present. In any case, the very issues which are usually thought of as automatically part of the remit of a federal parliament involve important moral, and financial, considerations. It is central to the case for independence that Scotland ought to manage her own foreign affairs. And it will be essential financially to escape involvement in England's profligate defence policy.

So it is, then, that Scottish nationalists seek independence for Scotland; an independence which will give a Scottish Government complete control over Scottish affairs; an independence which will enable Scotland to rethink her relationship with England and to establish official contacts with other countries. It is said that independence would involve a return to an inward-looking and old-fashioned national sovereignty. But to say that is simply to give evidence of a wilful refusal to look at relationships amongst small countries outside Britain. One thinks of the arrangements which have been made amongst the Scandinavian countries in this context. The point is that any such worthwhile relationship depends on the existence of sovereignty on both sides. For where that sovereignty exists, it establishes an equality amongst the parties concerned. And it is precisely the loss of this equality, as between Scotland and England, which is the most serious defect of the present system of government, and which to some degree or other would characterize any modification of the Union which falls short of establishing Scottish independence. Scotland may be smaller than England. But the close association which is bound to exist between the two nations in the future should not necessarily be regulated by any sort of assembly which reflects numerically this disparity in size. It must, on the contrary, be a genuine and equal partnership.

Opposition to self-government for Scotland often springs from an emotional view of Scotland's place in a great Empire. The Empire has gone now, but such attitudes linger. And if they linger amongst some Scots, it is true also that similar attitudes characterize the view of Scotland held by the English establishment. One way and another Scotland is of use to her political masters, whatever else they may pretend. At present, for example, Scotland provides a suitably 'remote' base for the Polaris submarines which will soon form the bulk of Britain's nuclear deterrent. This in itself will be one of the principal reasons why independence will be resisted by English politicians long after the bulk of the Scots have accepted the idea. And notwithstanding the cumulative effects of decades of bad management, Scotland makes a very valuable contribution to the United Kingdom economically.

I look forward to a time when the latter-day imperialists of London realize that Union between Scotland and England is as out of date as the British Empire, and that far more benefits of all kinds will accrue to the two nations when they are partners, each responsible for its own affairs.

8

In Defence of the United Kingdom

ESMOND WRIGHT

Let me begin by saying that it is not the case for the United Kingdom that has to be made, but the case against it. The United Kingdom exists. It has, at least for the last three centuries, given its varied peoples a higher material standard of living than any other country in the world outside the North American continent, and a happier, more peaceful, and more democratic political and social order than any other country in the world's history. It is not, of course, without need of improvement, for no system is perfect. But any case for basic constitutional change needs to be made and proven beyond doubt. It is the Scottish National Party which has to make, prove, and sustain that case, for it is the destruction of the U.K., as at present constituted, that it advocates. For my part, with all its imperfections, I prefer the present order—amended, revised, and improved—to the revolutionary notions of political and economic separatism.

In giving my reasons I shall rest my case largely on a rebuttal of the changes proposed by the S.N.P. In doing so I shall omit the economic arguments for the maintenance of the U.K.; they have been effectively marshalled elsewhere by Gavin McCrone in his admirable book, *Scotland's Future: The Economics of Nationalism*,[1] and by Professor K. J. W. Alexander in his companion essay in this book. I am aware that in omitting the economic arguments there is a danger that my own contribution will be a little like *Hamlet* without the Prince of Denmark, but I omit them on the Editor's instructions. In my view the economic arguments for the Union are overwhelming. No one of the government experts whom we have cross-examined in the meetings of the Select Committee on Scottish Affairs has even remotely suggested that there are any

[1] Oxford, 1969

103

economic grounds for the break-up of the economic framework of the U.K. And this, therefore, I am taking as read.

Since much of the S.N.P. case is not about economics but about emotions, I also run the risk of appearing to put up one emotion, that of Britain, against another, that of Scotland. Let me emphasize that to me these are not antithetical, but complementary. For 360 years the good Scot has been a good Briton. For long before that he was a better European than was the Englishman, and he has certainly been a good imperialist and internationalist. The British Empire could be even more accurately described as Scottish. So in putting a case for Britain I am not doing so as an alternative to Scotland, but as a case for the maintenance of the present connection. Why fly to other systems that we know not of? My first argument then is itself emotional. I believe the present in all its imperfections is a superior system to the alternative put forward by the S.N.P.

My second argument is historical: the U.K. is a fact and a product of history. It has existed as a union of the thrones since 1603, when a Scottish king, whose descendants still rule, went hot-foot to London and returned for only one brief visit. An ex-leader of the Scottish National Party, Professor Douglas Young of St. Andrews, now teaching classics in Canada, has said repeatedly 'what a pity it was that King James VI and I did not stay at home and send viceroys to London, Cardiff, and Dublin.' This is, of course, a quite unhistoric view, and it was the last thing in James's mind. England was much wealthier than Scotland and was the goal of his long contriving. It was Elizabeth's London the king aimed at, in a strong and salutary awareness of the blessings that come from unity. The same processes were at work in the Spain of Ferdinand and Isabella, and in contemporary France.

James VI was acceptable to the English because he was a Protestant and because he was Elizabeth's named heir. For their part, the Scots accepted his migration because he was a Scot, and because the inherited prize was in any case a very glittering one. And it was the real union of the two kingdoms that the king consciously sought. He proposed, in fact, to do with Scotland what Henry VIII had done with Wales. His native country would, he hoped, 'with time become but as Cumberland and Northumberland and those other remote and northern shires'. He meant it to be a total union, a single king, a single law, and a single Church, 'all manners and statutes welded into one as they are all one body under one head', and he declared:

> The union of these two princely houses is nothing comparable to the union of two ancient and famous kingdoms . . . if we were to look no higher than to natural and physical reasons, we may easily be persuaded of the great benefits that by that union do redound to the whole island. If twenty thousand men is a strong army, is not forty thousand a double the stronger army? . . . Do we not remember that this kingdom was divided into seven little kingdoms? And is it not now the stronger by their union? And hath not the union of Wales to England added a greater strength thereto? Hath not God first united these . . . kingdoms both in language and religion and similitude of manners? Yes, hath he not made us all in one island, compassed by one sea?

The events of 1603 have been buttressed by the whole of our subsequent history. The union of the thrones became in 1707 a union of the parliaments, and under the terms of the Act the complete freedom of Scots law, education, and Kirk was guaranteed, as it had not been by the Scottish Stuarts. The Union was, of course, carefully manufactured on both sides. Each side used bribery. It was part of the process of diplomatic negotiation well into the nineteenth century and so—again—our contemporary emotion about it is historically irrelevant. Each side needed the other. The English wanted to deny to the old enemy France a base in Scotland at the climax of a long war against Louis XIV; and rightly. The Scots, after the Darien failure, wanted to enjoy some of the boom of England's empire—from which they were excluded by the Navigation Acts of 1660 and 1663; and with equal justice. England's wealth was clearly due to her overseas trade and her prosperity was assured by the string of Atlantic colonies, from Newfoundland to the Caribbean, which supplied her with sugar, tobacco, and raw materials and held out the promise of markets for her manufactured goods. She was very much wealthier than Scotland; her population was some six millions against Scotland's one million; her land taxes yielded £2m, Scotland's £3,600. In contrast with England, Scotland's agricultural methods were primitive, her trade small and very vulnerable, her capital resources and products meagre. So she naturally wanted a share in the New World and in the new society.

Each country was prepared, in exchange for the benefits of the Union, to vote her own sovereign parliament out of existence and to establish a new parliament of the United Kingdom. (It is not nearly widely enough realized that England now has no parliament of her own, and in that sense she is as 'unfree' and 'unsovereign' as Scotland.) And so the deal was made. It was made by, it is true, a minority of Scots. If Scottish 'public opinion'—or English, for that matter—had been consulted, the deal would probably not have been made. This is not but to say that here, as so often, a minority were wiser than the majority; referenda are not automatic guides to wisdom. To use the argument about 'who bribed whom' in 1707 is to ignore the vast merits of the union that was accomplished. It would be equally absurd to judge the state of Israel by the nature of the deal that was made with Dr. Weizmann in 1916, which led to the Balfour Declaration, or to judge Czechoslovakia by the promise made by President Wilson to Masaryk in 1918. However accomplished, the union of the parliaments, like the union of the crowns, became—happily—a fact of history.

The history of neither country since 1707 can be seen in separation. Glasgow made the Clyde and the Clyde made Glasgow: but Glasgow made the Clyde in order that the tobacco, and later the cotton, of the (now British) colonies could get more quickly to its doors, and the profits from them more quickly into its pockets. By 1775 half the tobacco imports into Britain came to Glasgow, and half her exports to continental Europe went from Glasgow. In 1707 Glasgow was a 'dear green place', a little country town beside an undredged river fordable on foot; and its population was 12,000. In 1807 it was a major city and port with an open channel to the sea; and its population was over 70,000. The fine houses of the tobacco lords were a product of the Union. And so were the Scottish trading banks. 'Since St. Mungo catched herrings in the Clyde,' said Bailie Nicol Jarvie of Glasgow, 'what was ever like to gar us flourish like the sugar and tobacco trade? Will anybody tell me that and grumble at a treaty that opened us a road west-awa' yonder?' These developments made possible the exploitation of Scotland's resources of coal and iron. The Carron works were opened in 1759, on an Englishman's initiative and with English plant and artisans; by 1806 there were twenty-nine blast furnaces in Scotland. James Watt began life in Glasgow, but prospered much more in Birmingham in partnership with an Englishman. In

1787 John Gladstone, a Highlander, exchanged a business partnership at Leith for one in Liverpool, and so William Ewart Gladstone was born a Highland Liverpudlian. Moreover, from the very outset of the Union, the West of Scotland was morbidly afraid of its breakup: afraid in 1715 and still more in 1745. It was as prompt in '45 to bribe the Highland army away from the city as it had been to attract the English forty years before. And on the east coast, there grew up the New Town of Edinburgh, with one of the finest situations of any city in Europe, essentially a creation of the Act of Union. Edinburgh's golden age, like Dublin's, in painting, architecture, philosophy, literature, music and poetry, as well as theology, political economy, and applied science, was a direct outcome of the union; so were its prosperity and its fructifying new contacts and opportunities.

And it should be stressed that neither in 1603 nor in 1707 was this a conquest by an occupying power. There was no tyranny and no interference with freedom. The main pillars of the Scottish establishment, law, Church, education, were not only preserved, but guaranteed. Indeed, the very sound and imagery of Scotland that is expressed in its folk culture, its tradition and its lore, its pipes and drums, are a product of the world after 1707. Until General Wade built his roads, the north was seen as barbarous and backward by Lowlanders as well as by Sassenachs. Of the Scottish regiments only seven were raised before 1707 and all these, in fact, in the years between 1660 and 1690. They did not come into being to defend Scotland against England; on the contrary, they were raised and paid for in England itself. The Scotland of legend and of song was a product of the late eighteenth and early nineteenth centuries, and it was in particular the product of Sir Walter Scott's imagination—and of his publisher's pressures upon him. It was this image that was sold to George IV, and it was cemented thereafter by the romanticism that produced Balmoral.

It is, of course, possible from this long story to select ugly and less happy episodes and to lament them: the Victorian slums of Glasgow and Edinburgh, though some of these were as much an Irish as a Scottish phenomenon; the Clearances, overwhelmingly of Scots by other Scots; a tendency to anglicization in the south-east of Scotland, matching the complementary scotticization of the north-east of England, so that by this time few north-country Englishmen seem unable to claim a Scottish grandmother. But in fact, Scottish nationalism as we know it, an awareness of the existence of a Scottish people conscious of their unity and living in an identifiable area, was a product first of the Union and then of Sir Walter Scott. Until then there were in Scotland at least two nations, Highland and Lowland. The massacre of Glencoe in 1692 was the result of an order, not from England, but from a Scottish Lowland administration. The two areas were distinct in language —Gaelic and Lallans—in religion, and in their way of life. Most Highlanders were Jacobite and Catholic; the Lowlanders were far more in sympathy with the north of England than with the Highlands. And insofar as there came changes in the Highlands in the eighteenth and nineteenth centuries, they came from the steady penetration by Lowland sons with their Presbyterian faith. 'Have you no music, no singing, no dancing, now at your marriages?' asked a lover of Gaelic speech and custom on a visit to the Hebrides in 1899. The good wife replied:

> May the possessor keep you! You are a stranger in Lewis or you would not ask. It is long since we abandoned these foolish ways. In my young days there was hardly a house in Ness where there was not two or three who could play the pipes or the fiddle. . . . A blessed change came over the place. . . . The good men and the ministers who arose did away with the songs and the stories, the music and the dancing. . . . They made the people break and burn their pipes and fiddles.

As Celtic culture dwindled it was overlaid by Calvinist austerity. Moreover, insofar as there was in Scott's day a single nation in Scotland, it still sought ever closer identity with London and prospered from it, just as the twentieth-century nationalism of Ulster was, and remains, intensely pro-British. It is too often assumed that Scottish patriotism is necessarily anti-English; there was in the eighteenth century Glasgow of James Watt and Adam Smith and in the Edinburgh of Principal Robertson and Walter Scott no such wish for separation. Pride in Scotland then connoted an equal pride in Union. Burns himself was a champion of the Union and of the British Navy. It was for the Dumfries Volunteers that he wrote in 1795 'Be Britain still to Britain true among ourselves united'. 'Rule Britannia' was the work of a Scotsman, Thomson; it was Thomas Campbell of Glasgow who wrote in praise of 'Ye Mariners of England'.

Nor was the prosperity that arose from the English connection limited to the homeland. It was reflected in the Scottish families who saw in the Empire a ladder of opportunity and adventure. The history of British India is sonorous with names like Macpherson and Metcalf, Elphinstone and Dalhousie; so is the history of Africa with Mungo Park and David Livingstone; the true founder of Canadian federalism was John Macdonald, born and raised in Glasgow. And it is not the fault of the 'wicked English' that in the nineteenth and twentieth centuries Scottish investors sent their money to those places where it has brought the highest returns. Names like Jardine-Mathieson are bound up with Britain's role in Asia. In 1884 *Blackwood's Magazine* commented:

> For a small country like Scotland to be able to spare, even for a time, tens of millions sterling, is one of the most striking paradoxes in the history of commerce. The Scotch, of all people in the world, are supposed to be best able to take care of themselves and their money. Wherever a passable honest penny can be earned they will not be far to seek; and yet it has come to this with them, that they will face almost any risk for the sake of the difference between 4 per cent at home and 4½ per cent across the Atlantic.

The Scottish American Investment Company was founded in 1873 and is still going strong. The Matador Land Company was the most famous and most profitable of the American cattle companies, and its roots were in Dundee. The Swan Investment Company was fundamental to the early development of Texas and the American west. Arizona copper sent home £6 million in dividends between 1901 and 1921. The development of the western United States would not have been possible without Scottish capital and this came, not from the landed aristocracy, but from Scottish industry, from the flax and jute mills of Dundee, the thread mills of Paisley, and from heavy engineering on the Clyde, all of them direct products of the Union. The failure of Scotland to invest in itself and its wish to seek profits elsewhere is not a new phenomenon. What was striking in the nineteenth century was that there was an opportunity for thrift, and willingness to take risks in investment. Obviously a fraction of this investment in the American west would have done much for the Highlands and the Borders; but the fact remains that by their own choice the nineteenth-century Scots *entrepreneurs* were more distinguished for their shrewdness than for their patriotism.

Scotland's history since 1707 is the story of her contribution towards the history of Great Britain, and it is a proud and remarkably successful one. The U.K. built up the greatest empire the world has ever seen and the mightiest sea-power until the emergence of those super-powers of today, the U.S.A. and the U.S.S.R. Two small islands in the northern sea became the greatest trading nation on the face of the earth, the pioneer in the first industrial and agricultural revolution of the modern age, a leading scientific and inventing power, with the finest universities in Europe, and with London as the financial capital of the world—as it still is. This was an empire strong enough and resilient enough to survive Lord North and the loss of the American colonies. There is no reason whatever why we should not take pride in this splendid past and no reason why the decline of the Imperial idea and the period of inept and bureaucratic government should mean a loss of nerve. It is fashionable to be cynical about the Union, the Empire, the imagery of the past, and even the Crown itself. Yet Great Britain could still have a splendid future. She is still rich and very productive; still highly skilled, enterprising, and inventive; still in the van of the new industrial revolution, of electronics, computers, petrochemicals, and all the science-based industries.

Is Scottish Nationalism in fact a side-product of the decline of empire? Do Scots want to desert England now that the possessions have gone? Let them think very carefully before they risk a drastic shrinking of their fields of opportunity. Dead the Imperial idea is, but we still have access to Canada, Australia, New Zealand, South Africa. Scots would expect this to continue. They still seek fortunes —some of them considerable—in London and the Midlands. Of all the peoples of Britain the Scots have the greatest practical gifts, of shrewdness, thrust, hard work. It would be a pity indeed to confine all this energy within the boundaries of a far northern country with a population of only five millions. Already there are great hopes for the future of the Clyde estuary, with its deep-water advantages and situation, and large-scale British and American investment is planned. If the Clyde project is to be as big as it promises to be, it will mean yet another lease of life for the Clyde, such as it gained in earlier generations from sugar and tobacco, then cotton, then coal, steel and ships. It will, like earlier developments, take all the energy, invention, and initiative of the United Kingdom—and more. Separatism and customs barriers, strident parochialism, high rates and taxes will do nothing to help. It will call for attractive private housing, a friendly welcome, and tax incentives on a very big scale.

The Union is a fact of history and it has brought to both countries a high standard of living. I believe that in Union lies hope for both countries for the future also.

But the S.N.P. would replace the union by seeking to create a separate Scottish kingdom. One assumes it would be a kingdom—some of their voices are republican. Let me suggest some of the major risks of any such development: I can see at least eight.

One, it is a parochial, inward-looking movement in an age whose main characteristic is its internationalism. Of course no one can deny the strength of roots. We love the place where we were born and never forget that love. Without it, our powers of imagination and perhaps the most deeply felt and most spiritual forces within us would be arid and bleak. A sense of 'apartness' is preserved in songs, poetry, and folk-lore, and reinforced, in Scotland's case, by her own systems of law, religion, and education. When things go wrong the Scot, like the Welsh, has an identity-kit available and can fit easily into it. The Clydesider, unlike the Tynesider or the Yorkshireman, can express his local grievances through nationalism.

But patriotism—and it is not the monopoly of any one party—is not necessarily parochialism. Some of the most fervent nationalists have been, in fact, imperialists seeking to create larger systems rather than smaller ones. Bismarck was a Prussian patriot, but he created a federal German Empire; Cavour, Prime Minister of Piedmont, the only modernized and the most prosperous of the Italian states in his day, dreamed of the unification of the whole peninsula, although all of it south of Tuscany was economically very backward and much of it ruled by Austria. He knew that Piedmont could never be a world power, but that Italy could. The great and successful nationalist movements of the nineteenth century, led by fervent patriots, were not separatist at all, but movements for unification, often federal. The intense pride and sense of identity of the Texan has been in no way diminished by the absorption of the Lone Star State into the greater union, and

Stalin's Georgia is no less itself for having become part of the U.S.S.R. Brittany could patently only be weakened if it—or any other region—broke away from France. All the great nations of the world, France, Spain, U.S.A., U.S.S.R., Germany, Italy, have been built as the U.K. was built—by fusing the regions together. We are too apt, on hearing the word 'nationalism', to see it as a viewpoint of smaller nations or smaller regions.

And we are too apt to assume that the core of the sense of identity is political—the common life lived by a group of people, sharing history, a common language, and common traditions. But it is doubtful if it is politics that taps the spirit. Was it Czechoslovakia or the particular beauty of the Moldau that inspired Smetana? Was it England or the beauty of the Lake District that moved Wordsworth? We can name a host of American poets and writers who have voiced their pride in the United States, but what stirred Robert Frost were the vistas of the New England landscape, its little red schoolhouses and its tall white spires; what moved Stephen Foster or S. V. Benet was the American Deep South and what William Faulkner captures in his novels is his own understanding of Oxford, Mississippi. In an age made international by satellites and by mass communication, it is not the American South that is communicable, but Yoknapatawpha County; it is not Scotland that is understood, but Tannochbrae. Andrew Cruickshank is far more significant than Mrs Ewing or Hugh MacDiarmid.

Secondly, it is at this point that one is moved to question whether there is a genuine Scottish Nationalism at all. It is hard to prove in a literary, or in a geographic, sense. Much of the 'Scots language' is synthetic and, as with much of the writing of Hugh MacDiarmid, contrived; indeed, where the spoken word is concerned, much of it is shared on both sides of Cheviot. Even if one accepts that the Lallans is the native Scottish language rather than a dialect, and if one accepts that it is the living language—both highly debatable theses—it is not the language of the majority of the Scottish people; any more than is Gaelic. Unlike Welsh Nationalism, Scottish Nationalism is not a movement of linguistic or cultural identity. The politics of the S.N.P. are not the politics of Gaeldom; their roots are in the Lowlands, not in the Celtic areas; their impact on the Highlands has been negligible thus far. In any event a movement towards devolution cannot be halted at

Carter Bar or Cheviot. Orkney and Shetland have recently indicated that they have no natural links with Caithness and no especial liking for Edinburgh. Geographically, there are sharper contrasts between Orkney and the Borders, or between the Western Isles and Fife, than there are between most regions of England. There is in Scotland no basic natural unity of economics or of race, of religion or of culture. And if a victorious S.N.P. were to claim independence for the area at present labelled Scotland, what would be the limits of secession? A Scottish Government which expected Orkney and Shetland to share water and police authorities with the mainland, as St. Andrew's House directs them to do, would command no more sympathy than does the present Secretary of State. Does the future of the Borders rest with England or with Scotland? How far is prosperous Edinburgh prepared to go in carrying the huge debt of Glasgow? It should constantly be borne in mind that U.K. subventions to B.E.A. and British Rail in Scotland would cease. Indeed, both would cease to exist. English European Airways would presumably operate only to termini in Glasgow and Edinburgh—if not Newcastle and Carlisle—thankfully abandoning the heavily subsidized routes to the north. Cunard and naval orders for hitherto Clyde-built ships would go to Belfast, Barrow, or Tyneside, and there would be no one to stop English firms—or American ones—pulling out of Scottish branches if the economic climate in a free Scotland worsened.

This raises the fundamental point. The case for Scottish separatism is based on the belief that Scotland is a nation state and that the boundary lines of nation and state are identical. Some of their own leaders take pride in claiming that they want an independent Scotland to sit at the United Nations between Saudi Arabia and Senegal—apparently assuming that either of these has any influence there whatsoever. They forget that it was disruptive nationalism which destroyed the stability of central Europe and that the seeds of Hitlerism and irredentism were sown at the Peace Settlement of 1919. The repeated model they use for an Independent Scotland is Norway, forgetting the fact that Norway has none of our industrial problems because it has no industrial base, and no huge city like Glasgow to subsidize; forgetting that its money market is not in Oslo, but in London; and forgetting how completely dependent it is on its own relations with the Scandinavian bloc, with Europe, and with Canada. But why choose Norway as prototype? Why not Eire where, since its independence, its wages rates have been approximately half those of the U.K., where there is only a very rudimentary Welfare State, and where since independence its export of people to the U.K. has increased sharply? The true parallel ought to be with Ulster, which faces the same problems of race and religion as does Scotland, where unemployment is much higher than in Scotland, and where, nevertheless, nationalist sentiment is firmly pro-British. If we need to look for parallels elsewhere why not Texas; or Bavaria, where Franz Joseph Strauss finds it possible to marry pride in Bavaria with pride in the greater unity of Germany; or with the Mezzogiorno, which is booming because of the aid given to it by the larger unity of Italy; or with Sicily, which became completely autonomous after the war, but now seeks closer links with Rome again?

But the case against the identity of state and nation is fundamental. No one questions the reality or the depth of Scottish national feeling. But why, in as sophisticated and highly educated a union as this, should this mean separate statehood? If Scotland is to be fully politically independent, are there to be separate customs and excise systems, and if so, a separate tax system too? Does this mean passports? What happens to those who are literally British with both Scots and English parents? If Scots become aliens, will they be allowed into England? Will they yield precedence to Kenyan Asians who have British passports? What does it mean to say, as the S.N.P. did at its 1969 Conference at Oban, that the entry of immigrants would be related to the requirements of labour and available housing? Would Scots in England have to choose citizenship, and if they chose Scottish, would they then be asked to leave? It is, of course, easy to say that the English are tolerant and sweet-natured and that there is no restriction of Irish immigrants into England, but nationalism in one part of the U.K. could produce counter-nationalism elsewhere and there can be no guarantee that it would not. A sovereign Scottish parliament means a sovereign English parliament, which no one is yet demanding, but which could become equally xenophobic.

It is too often contended that healthy nationalism is at the centre of healthy internationalism. This is, in fact, historically untrue. Nationalism, and the quest to align state and nation, has been the truly disruptive factor in modern history and it has produced more frontier clashes, and in the end world wars, than any other single cause. In a world that is becoming more and more an international one, and in which indeed the U.K. is itself too small, the case for separatism is difficult to sustain. Nationalist voices tend to be those of repeated protest and frustration, and the policies that they voice are less and less relevant to our times. The great internationalists of our age, Norman Angell, Robert Cecil, and Count Coudenhove-Kalergi, have never been deceived into the pretence that nationalism is anything but the enemy of genuine internationalism.

Third, it is clear that while S.N.P. policy is for total separation from England—and indeed there is no other reason for their existence as a party—many who at present vote for them do not in fact want complete independence. But in the content of the rest of their policy the Scottish Nationalists are extraordinarily varied. At the 1968 Conference, they passed a resolution confirming that they were against the principle of party whips either at local or central government levels. Mr. Keith Bovey said a man's first duty was to his principles, and he hoped that no member of the S.N.P. would ever become lobby fodder. 'We believe that this system can be made to work with no sacrifice of efficiency. Representatives of the party can work on a consensus of opinion among themselves', he said. 'No S.N.P. representative at any level has the right to bully any other into voting for something in which he does not believe.'

It is clear that they are, of course, a radical party. Arthur Donaldson says that he expects that a Scottish Government would take in all Scotland's radicals, and Gordon Wilson, the party's National Secretary, thinks that if they ever got power they would be a radical party like the Social Democrats of Norway or Sweden. Mrs. Ewing's nationalism is plainly rooted deep in socialism and pacifism. At their Conference in 1968 they said 'the land and all natural resources belong to the people (that means the government) and will be held subject to the . . . control of the proposed National Assembly.' But it is also clear that the party would split up into right and left once the battle was won. This became very clear at the Oban Conference in 1969. One of their policy statements was described by their own supporters as 'straight out of Karl Marx'. They have already expelled their own 1320 Club on the right and the Communist Hugh MacDiarmid on the left. They are not a party but a revolutionary movement with many strands. As a result their policies are extraordinarily mixed. It seems, from their policy document 'S.N.P. and You', that they would save the Argylls yet disband the Scottish regiments; they opposed the Transport Act yet favour the nationalization of transport; they oppose centralization, but they want to make housing and education the complete responsibility of the U.K. central government; they claim that Scotland loses money to the U.K. yet disclaim that Scotland wants to be a parasite on England.

Many of their *obiter dicta* about maximum land holdings, the break-up of assets and compulsory purchase of the land are, of course, extremely controversial. They have made no contribution as yet to the basic arguments of today over democracy and participation. On defence policy in particular they have been a party with many and inconsistent voices, though it seems clear that they will want no foreign bases on Scottish soil. The Polaris base on the Holy Loch, the Naval base at Rosyth, and the R.A.F. stations at Leuchars, Kinloss, and Turnhouse will all go. But in some mysterious way Scotland will have an Army, Air Force, and Navy of her own and a force to be put at the disposal of the United Nations. There has been no estimate of what it costs to buy or build just one jet fighter, much less to equip an infantry brigade. But what is curious here is a total indifference to the conspicuous military tradition of Scotland. They are happy to have the pipes and drums, the kilt and the Glengarry, to have their party ceilidhs and to exploit a martial imagery, but a coherent defence or foreign policy it is impossible to find.

Fourth, a more serious criticism, is that all of this is simply irrelevant to the very real Scottish problems of the day: how to stimulate Scottish industry and research; how to widen the middle-class character of the country and provide those private houses and amenities that will attract economic managerial talent; how to develop the growth points on scientific and electronic development; what to do about rents and rates which have nothing to do with England. Here, the Scottish Nationalist Party, on its record, has voted repeatedly against all basic proposals for change. Mr. Norman Buchan, the Labour Under-Secretary of State, has described their attitude as 'un-Scottish, indeed anti-Scottish'. In the four aspects of Scottish life most closely affected, the Highlands, steel and shipbuilding, the new growth and technological industries, and the universities and other centres of research, we still need to draw upon U.K. resources—at least—and remain vitally linked to Britain in terms of expansion.

Fifth, S.N.P.'s policy is one which is indifferent to the need for security in the modern world. The age of the nuclear deterrent has been an age that has seen many 'bush fire' wars. Since 1945 there have been at least fifty outbreaks of war across the globe, and in a nuclear age it is the little countries that are at risk—Israel and Czechoslovakia, Cuba and Singapore. How could Scotland alone possibly defend herself? Because she would have no foreign policy and defence force, it does not mean that she would not need them, nor does it mean that she would have lost her attraction as a base for attack on England. Indeed, the S.N.P. has moved steadily, as it has grown in popularity, towards a total abnegation on the defence side. No responsible politician can accept defence proposals that are in fact simply total powerlessness dressed up as policy. And the whole question of defence and foreign policy has very recently gained a new urgency. The action in Czechoslovakia, reports of Russian activity in the North Sea and the North Atlantic as well as the Mediterranean, rouse new fears over Soviet ambitions and strategy. To this the S.N.P. shows a total indifference.

Sixth, in some fields Scotland is, in fact, too much independent already. She is completely autonomous in law, education, and religion in terms of the Act of Union, and no one is seeking to change this. She has her own municipal authorities who are free to raise their rates and to have rate poundages and systems differing widely from those in England. She is free to build as many council houses as she likes, and has a far higher proportion of them, and a far more rigid division between council tenants and owner-occupiers, than in England. She has her own television authorities, her own S.T.U.C., her own political parties separate from those of England. She has her own Secretary of State and Under-Secretaries, and her own civil servants, based in Edinburgh. Even the Scottish Boards of gas, coal, and electricity are independent and autonomous. Yet what do most Scots grumble about? High rates and their effect on prices; poor television programmes; high prices of fuel and transport; and, currently, a dispute over membership of the teaching profession. No one of these has anything to do with the English connection and, indeed, Scotland would benefit greatly if prices in the nationalized industries were standardized over the whole of the U.K. and if regional boards ceased to be financially autonomous.

Seventh, if, at the next election the S.N.P. won a majority of Scottish seats, and went on to declare Scotland independent by verdict of the 'majority vote', that would be a revolution, a U.D.I. It is, therefore, a revolutionary party. And revolutions have a way of generating their own momentum. No matter what sort of state the S.N.P. promise to establish, we have no guarantee that revolution will end with a simple declaration of independence. The party itself would split into warring factions; other parties and interests would still exist, many of them still supporting the Union. Would they be traitors? There would be a frightening struggle for power. Where would it end? In France, the well-meaning milk-and-water liberal aristo, Lafayette, gave way to Robespierre, and Robespierre to Napoleon; there followed Waterloo, and the restoration of the Bourbons. France was very lucky that Napoleon was a great man and a brilliant administrator, but the French Revolution was not started by people who wanted an imperial despot in place of an inefficient and rather stupid king. Kerensky ended in Stalin; Weimar ended in Hitler. Any unconstitutional move in Scotland would at best considerably frighten the middle classes, landowners, taxpayers, and prospective investors and developers, especially from outside. No one can foretell what might follow.

Eighth and finally, revolution in Scotland would force into being that other great imponderable—an English parliament and an English nationhood. There is no way of knowing what a sovereign, free, English parliament (which no one is demanding) would be like; but it would probably start its existence with a deep sense of resentment. One thing is certain, there would be no Scottish interests represented there, no one to prevent orders from going to the Tyne instead of the Clyde, no one to protest as branches of English firms pulled out of Scotland. The S.N.P. expect that it would be co-operative. If they are right, and the English are as generous, tolerant, and grudge-free as all that, why are they seeking so unnecessary and arbitrary a separation from them? It is more likely that a suddenly independent England would turn her back on a far northern market of only five millions and look more and more towards Europe and the U.S.A., worrying vaguely about defence and the security of her northern frontier, and being forced to act if it were ever menaced. And if the S.N.P. now protest that they do not favour customs barriers and a fortified frontier, how do we know what an English parliament will favour? The Nationalists cannot possibly give us any reassurance on either of these points—the nature and outcome of a Scottish revolution, and the nature and reactions of a sovereign English parliament. They *are* imponderables and will remain so until we experience them. A vote for the S.N.P., therefore, is a great 'leap in the dark'. I hope fervently, for all our sakes and for Scotland's future, that it is never taken.

The most serious charge of all against the S.N.P. is the poverty of its constructive and long-term thinking. It is firmly against the U.K., against the Labour Government and St. Andrew's House, against Conservatism, against N.A.T.O. What is it for? A totally separate Scotland which it has not yet defined either geographic-ally, economically, or politically. It voices, in other words, the politics of frustration, and the core of its nationalism would seem to be xenophobia, dislike of the outsider. It is no accident that Hugh MacDiarmid gives his recreation in *Who's Who?* as 'anglo-phobia'.

The basic trouble with a nationalism that is seeking wilfully to destroy a system that is working perfectly well and to establish something altogether smaller, is that it turns in upon itself, becomes parochial and stiff-necked, and sees the world outside as alien, enemy, different. The basic truth about the United Kingdom rests in the fact that since 1707 we have built in these islands a unique political system, unmatched elsewhere, a federal society of English, Scots, Welsh, and Irish and nowadays many more, that is nevertheless a single centralized political system, a working parliamentary democracy that can even now curb and control an over-mighty executive through the House of Commons, and through the fact that ministers must be members of parliament. This union of equals and the energy it released gave our tiny islands a standard of living to which their natural resources in no way entitled them, and a place in history alongside the Romans themselves. We have lived, since 1945, through a traumatic period of loss of empire, loss of status, loss of pride. But the pride and status at least can be regained, and the society and the system remain unique, flexible, and workable. We must change the political character of the union only if we genuinely believe that the present weaknesses in it are of so essentially fundamental a sort, so intrinsically related to our decline as a world power and an economic force, that they are the cause of our 'failure'. I do not believe this to be the case, and I find nothing in the S.N.P. phrases to convince me.

This is not to say that I see no need for any form of devolution. On the contrary, I would welcome help from some sort of Scottish Assembly, sitting in Edinburgh, to discuss purely Scottish legislation, perhaps seeing Acts through their earlier stages before being finally debated by the U.K. parliament. But final proposals on the composition and selection of such an Assembly cannot be made until we know what the new shape of local government is to be. We must be very careful, whatever we decide on, to avoid a proliferation of bureaucracies. But this is premature and cannot be decided until the Wheatley Report appears. Meantime, for me, I prefer the U.K. to the dangerous, emotional and ill-considered notions of separatism.

9

Independence: The Economic Issues

DAVID SIMPSON

At a recent branch meeting of the Scottish National Party a resolution was passed after a debate to the effect that an undue preoccupation with applied economics was causing a decline in interest in politics in Scotland. To some extent this resolution reflects the increasing confusion in the public mind and, indeed, the general boredom with the welter of phoney statistics and half-truths which are being bandied about by the unionist parties in the present discussion of the question of independence for Scotland. It is fair to say that the economic aspect of independence does worry very many people in Scotland. It is also true that there is no real foundation for such concern. Nevertheless, one has to recognize as a political fact that such concern does exist.

There seems to have grown up in Scotland in the 250-odd years since the Union began a tremendous sense of dependence upon England. It has reached the point that most people in Scotland are quite surprised to discover that there are other countries which are even smaller than Scotland and which still have a higher standard of living, and to discover that political independence does not have such dramatic economic repercussions as they often imagine. Such a feeling of dependence in an economic sense upon England has, of course, been fostered both consciously and unconsciously by the experience of post-war years. In this time we have seen the role of government in the economy expand enormously as the government has accepted more and more responsibility for a wide range of economic activity. Since the government is located in Westminster this has inevitably meant that the people in Scotland have looked towards Westminster for a solution of their grievances, whether these be questions of poverty or of unemployment. And since the war it has become an

121

accepted part of political life that people in Scotland should put to the Westminster Government demands which almost invariably take the form that more money should be spent on some project or another. And so Westminster has come to be regarded as the great pork-barrel which provides for the people of Scotland an endless supply of good things which are to be had only for the asking. Perhaps a more appropriate metaphor would be that of the Westminster Government as a broken-down vending machine. One puts in one's money in the form of taxation and nothing happens, so one has to keep on kicking the machine until one gets a response. Much of the frustration now revealing itself in current political life reflects the fact that people are finding that they have to kick harder and longer in order to get a response.

It is difficult to exaggerate the importance of this attitude of *dependence*, an attitude which runs very deeply throughout Scotland. It is, indeed, reflected in the attitudes of the two unionist parties, Tory and Labour, who vie with each other on public platforms in boasting of the subsidies which their governments at Westminster have provided at one time or another to the people of Scotland. Even were one to accept the validity of their claims (which I do not), the most startling thing about this attitude is the fact that people should take it for granted that subsidies of this kind are something of which the recipients should be proud. It does no credit to the Scottish tradition of independence and personal responsibility that we should have got ourselves into a position of willingness to accept the idea that we are to be permanent recipients of the generosity of the Westminster Government. This is nothing more than the philosophy of the begging-bowl, a philosophy which in the long run has always corrupted those who are the receivers of the charity as well as those who are the givers. It is my opinion, an opinion not contradicted by the available evidence, that we in Scotland have contributed at least as much to the Westminster Government in the form of taxes and other government revenues as we have ever received from it in the form of government expenditures. But what concerns me for the moment is not the actual balance of revenues and expenditures so much as the attitude which lies behind the idea of the Westminster Government being a charitable dispenser of unearned benefits, a role which the representatives of the two unionist parties have been happy to adopt.

As a corollary of this attitude, one of the oldest arguments which has been advanced against the idea of political independence is that, whilst this might be an attractive ambition, Scotland is too small a country to afford it. This original objection is, of course, easily dismissed by looking at the number of countries in Europe alone which are smaller than Scotland: countries such as Norway and Denmark and Finland which have a standard of living at least as high as Scotland's. It is also worth remembering that Switzerland has a standard of living far superior to that of Scotland, though its population is only slightly larger.

Secondly, there is the argument that Scotland is too poor a country to stand on its own: measured by average income, however, Scotland is one of the top twenty countries in the world, and there are literally scores of poorer countries which manage to be politically independent. Recently these types of argument have become so discredited that we no longer hear the once familiar parrot-cry that independence will be 'economic suicide'. Instead, more sophisticated voices have joined the debate on the unionist side and, while their arguments have no more foundation than the older and cruder arguments, nevertheless, they do have a superficial plausibility, and therefore they must be dealt with. I shall consider these arguments one by one.

It is now generally conceded by economists that Scotland would have no trouble in surviving as a viable economic unit following political independence. What is still at issue is the question of the standard of living immediately following independence. It has been argued, for example, that an independent Scotland would lose the subsidies which are alleged to flow from the U.K. Exchequer at Westminster to Scotland. This argument depends, of course, on the existence of subsidies to Scotland over and above taxes which are paid by Scotland to the U.K. Treasury. So far, despite many promises from the Chief Secretary to the Treasury, we have as yet had no conclusive evidence from the Government,[1] who are the only people in a position to provide this information, to support the suggestion that Scotland is a net receiver of subsidies from the U.K. Government.

[1] Since this essay was prepared, the Treasury has issued a 'Scottish Budget.' Despite many flaws in this document, it does not make the mistake of claiming that Scotland is subsidized by England. No such regard for the facts has restrained the Government's interpretation of it to the press and public.

E

A related proposition, reiterated in a recent book,[1] is that a Scottish Government would either have to raise taxes or to borrow more in order to maintain existing levels of expenditure. Such an argument overlooks the point that a Scottish Government would have no need to maintain many items of spending at their present levels. For example, if defence expenditure per head were reduced to the level obtaining in N.A.T.O. Norway or neutral Switzerland, the resulting savings, together with other cuts in overseas expenditure, would be enough to avoid the necessity of any tax increases. This point was recognized by the same author in a recent article in *New Outlook*, where he wrote: 'If all this [S.N.P. policy] happened, Scotland would have no budgetary problem'.[2] It is important to emphasize that cutting defence expenditure does not mean shedding Scotland's share of responsibility in any European arrangements for collective defence. Defence expenditure per head in Norway, which is a member of N.A.T.O., stands at half the U.K. level. This simply reflects the pretensions of the U.K. government in maintaining a defence establishment which is obsolete and ineffective. In the last analysis, U.K. defence depends upon the Americans.

It has been suggested, secondly, that we should suffer the disadvantage of losing the political influence which Scotland is alleged to have in the Cabinet in making decisions about the allocation of industry and of government contracts. If there has been any influence exerted on Scotland's behalf within the Cabinet, then it is difficult to see what the results of this influence have been. The Northern Irish have no Minister in the Cabinet and twelve non-playing Members in the House. Yet they receive far more subsidies per head than the Scots do, and as Dr. McCrone shows, the rate of growth of employment in Northern Ireland in the post-war period has been three times as great as in Scotland.[3]

There is a further argument which suggests that outside the political framework of England, Scotland would not have the benefit of the legislation which attempts to divert industries from the south-east of England and sends them to development areas which include Scotland. Although this argument has a superficial

[1] G. McCrone, *Scotland's Future*, Oxford, 1969.
[2] G. McCrone, 'The Economics of Scottish Nationalism', *New Outlook*, November, 1968.
[3] G. McCrone, *Scotland's Future*, p. 18.

plausibility there are at least three basic flaws in it. First of all, even under the present arrangements the Board of Trade, which has the responsibility for the location of industry, has no particular reason to favour Scotland any more than any other development region such as the north-east of England or East Anglia. Therefore there is no reason why the Board of Trade should particularly wish to direct industry to Scotland even though it may wish to get it away from south-east England. The second flaw in this argument is that there is very little evidence that the principal instrument of the Board of Trade's diversionary policy, namely the issuing of Industrial Development Certificates, has had much influence in causing firms to relocate away from the south-east of England. This, at least, was the conclusion of the C.B.I. report which recently made a special study of the government's regional policy.[1] Then, thirdly, the fact of being independent does not mean that a country is prevented thereby from adopting whatever policies are thought necessary and desirable to promote industrial development. On the contrary, other European countries such as the Netherlands, Norway, and Denmark have been much more successful than has Scotland in attracting investment since the war, despite the absence of representation at Westminster. In this respect, it is worth mentioning that the much-vaunted U.K. 'regional' policy instruments may not be at all the most efficient way of attracting industry. There is a good case for arguing that a much more discriminating system of grants could be instituted, so that for any given level of expenditure a greater number of jobs could be created.

A further issue which must be considered in a politically independent Scotland is the question of trade relations with other countries, and notably with England. It is quite widely believed that an independent Scotland would somehow be separated in an economic sense both from England and from other countries. Nothing could be further from the truth. The S.N.P.'s explicit policy laid down in all its policy statements is that it would seek to negotiate a customs union with England. This would mean effectively continuing present arrangements so far as the free movement of goods and services across the border is concerned. Thus,

---

[1] *Regional Development and Distribution of Industry Policy*, London, 1968. See also R. C. Tress, 'Towards a New Regional Policy', *The Three Banks Review*, March, 1969.

the S.N.P. believes *not* in *separation* but in *co-operation* in the economic as well as in the political sphere. It is sometimes suggested in this connection that in establishing such a trading treaty with England, Scotland would be at a disadvantage in that the English market is evidently of considerable importance to us. While this is true, it overlooks the counter-balancing point that Scotland forms by no means a negligible market for English goods and that, therefore, England has a very similar interest in maintaining free and stable trading relationships with Scotland.

Another argument which is sometimes put forward is that, while all the trading arrangements which have been suggested are perfectly feasible, they would leave Scotland with no greater degree of independence than she has at the moment: such close trading links with England would leave virtually no freedom of manoeuvre so far as the control of our own economy is concerned. It is worth reflecting that, if this argument were true, then the unionists would have nothing to worry about; if Scotland were not really going to be a free agent after independence, unionists need not object to an independence which—on their argument—would change nothing. But, of course, the argument is a false one; and to see this we need look no further than across the Irish Sea. The Irish Republic is a country which is almost half Scotland's size and certainly has a very much lower average income. At the same time it is just as closely tied to England, in so far as its exports are concerned, as is Scotland. Despite this degree of trade dependence, the history of the last ten years shows that the Republic of Ireland has been able to pursue successfully policies of demand management and of industrial development which are independent of those being pursued in England and in the United Kingdom over this period. So, if the Irish can do it, Scotland which is both larger and richer can certainly do it. The recent experience of New Zealand shows, moreover, how rapidly a country can diversify its exports should the need arise; and indeed it would only be a healthy development if Scotland were to expand her exports to Europe and the United States and try to lessen her dependence on the markets of only one country.

Yet another argument which is sometimes put forward, a variant on the last one, is the suggestion that after independence Scotland would continue to experience exactly the same problems of economic policy which have afflicted the U.K. in the last ten to fifteen years: recurring balance of payments difficulties and problems of industrial relations. Factors in the recurring U.K. balance of payments crises since the war, however, are principally those which would *not* be likely to occur in an independent Scotland. In the United Kingdom there is a reserve currency which lends itself to periodic speculative attacks on the prevailing exchange rate; there is also, of course, the question of a very large U.K. Government expenditure abroad. Neither of these would be likely to be factors in an independent Scotland. This is not to say that we should never have balance of payments problems. It does mean, however, that we should be able to resolve them without the hysterical bursts of speculative panic leading to forced deflations and even devaluation which have been the experience of the United Kingdom. So far as labour relations are concerned, it is far less easy to predict the future. It is worthwhile pointing out, however, that it is probably easier to settle industrial differences in the environment of a small rather than a large country. Nevertheless, it cannot be denied that for rapid progress to be made there must be some reform of industrial relations in Scotland. But I should expect that this reform need not be directly dependent upon the issue of political independence and the extent to which it is achieved in the next few years.

When all of these arguments have been discussed until even a sceptic would be satisfied, there remains lurking in the back of the minds of most Scottish people the nagging doubt that after independence some dreadful thing will happen. Will there be unemployment? Will there be emigration? May there not be a falling standard of living? Shall we be able to afford to pay for the social services which we have come to take for granted? I shall consider these questions in turn. It is worth noting, however, that their expression is usually an indication of a basic insecurity on the part of the questioner, for the questions themselves do not seem based on any objective appraisal of probabilities. However, the fears are real enough and must therefore be considered. First of all, the social services: there are few things which one can be dogmatic about in politics, but it does seem quite safe to say that a Scottish Government would have no problems whatever in finding the revenues to pay to maintain the standards of social services as we enjoy them today.

On the question of unemployment, many people may think that

this will increase after independence. But, after all, is it likely that we should have to endure for ten years the levels of unemployment which have come to be accepted as normal in Scotland? Nor is it easy to imagine that we should have to endure under independence the levels of emigration which we have been forced to accept over the last ten or twenty years. And certainly, since 1964, or even earlier, the standard of living of the great majority of Scottish people has been stagnating, while for some sections of the community it has actually been falling. All these alleged difficulties which may befall Scotland are already with us, so what do we have to lose? Surely we cannot be any worse off, so far as these factors are concerned, than we are now? On the contrary, there is every indication that we shall be much better off.

Contrary to the view which is popularly fostered by the Tory and Labour parties, the standard of living in Scotland does not depend upon the generosity of the Westminster Government. It depends on exactly the same factors as does the standard of living of any other country: on the daily efforts, skill, and judgment of miners, school teachers, nurses, mechanics, salesmen, and bus conductors, and of every other working member of the community, as well as upon the stock of buildings and machinery and equipment which has been produced by our fathers and forefathers. Scotland's future standard of living will likewise depend upon our own efforts in the future. There is no reason to think that these efforts will grow less; indeed, there is considerable evidence to suggest that our efforts will be increased following independence, since people will feel that they have something worth working for.

This last point brings me to what I consider to be the overwhelming *economic* argument in favour of political independence. (Perhaps I should emphasize that I do not believe that the arguments for and against independence are primarily to be settled on economic grounds. But I do believe that there are some economic arguments in favour of independence and the one which I would now like to mention is the one which seems to me to be the most important.) Self-government is good, not just because it may lead to greater efficiency in running the Scottish economy: self-government is good as an end in itself because it means that people are *learning by doing*. This means that, if we take the responsibility for running our own affairs, then we as producers are likely to benefit from this responsibility, because in exercising it we make ourselves more efficient and become better able to do the job. I think that few people would disagree with this idea of the value of running one's own affairs. It is often argued against this, of course, that the gain to the individual in terms of the added responsibility may be more than offset by the losses which arise because of the lost advantages of centralized control. This is another way of saying that self-government may not be as good as good government. Whether or not this is true, it can hardly be denied that self-government is better than *bad* government, and the latter is the alternative which is facing us today.

People are, on the whole, willing to sacrifice a little independence or responsibility so long as they feel that those to whom they entrust the responsibility for running their affairs are making a competent job of it. However, the evidence has depressingly and repeatedly pointed to the opposite conclusion and disillusionment with the competence of administrators has become almost complete. There is a further tendency which has been recently recognized and which may also in part account for the desire of people to restore to themselves the responsibility for running their own affairs. This is the tendency towards the centralization of decision-making in the south-east of England which received the attention recently of the Scottish Council in a report entitled: *Centralization.* The subject of the report was the growing importance of London as the headquarters for many of the major activities of large companies and, indeed, of government departments. There is therefore a growing imbalance in Scotland, not only between the total number of jobs in relation to United Kingdom jobs, but also an imbalance in the quality of jobs. Jobs with any responsibility are increasingly to be obtained only outside Scotland. It is not difficult to see that this can have an extremely deleterious effect on the quality of life in Scotland and there are already signs of just such effects. Naturally, one of the immediate consequences of political independence would be a decentralization of decision-making. The head offices of nationalized industries and government departments would be located in Scotland within one hour's travelling time of the greater proportion of Scottish firms. This would be an immediate and tangible benefit of independence which is often overlooked, but which I think should not be underestimated.

A further advantage of political independence from the economic point of view is the fact that it would give us the instruments of control of our economy. For a long time now we have had inflicted on us various policies such as taxation of employment in services, and periodic restrictions on bank lending which, however appropriate they may have been for the south-east of England, have certainly never been appropriate for the Scottish economy. They have simply accelerated the trends in emigration and unemployment. In fact, the medicine which has been applied to the Scottish economy, so far from effecting a cure, has actually made the patient worse. Deflating the Scottish economy in the name of the U.K. balance of payments is about as appropriate as putting a starving man on a diet of bread and water to cure his neighbour's obesity. This fundamental criticism of the economic consequences of the union has been recognized by many economists. Nonetheless, there seems no sign that this has brought about any change in government policy. It seems that only the achievement of political independence will bring about a situation in which measures appropriate to the needs of the Scottish economy—that is the need for more jobs and not fewer jobs, for more investment and not less investment—will be satisfied by Scottish economic policies which are relevant to the Scottish economy. One has only to look at the many instruments by which a modern state now exercises control over its economy to see how totally the economy of Scotland is under the control of ministries in the Westminster Government. So far as the welfare of the Scottish economy is concerned, the Office of the Secretary of State is largely irrelevant. This was illustrated quite dramatically in the recent crisis at the Upper Clyde shipyards where the fate of almost 20,000 men's jobs was at stake. Negotiations over these jobs were between the shipbuilders and the Ministry of Technology. The Secretary of State's Office played no significant part in the negotiations. The Minister of Technology has made it perfectly clear that the Government in Westminster has no intention of continuing to make an open-ended commitment to subsidize Upper Clyde shipbuilders and that they will only extend further financial assistance if it is thought that this is going to bring about long-term viability of the company. This seems to me to be a perfectly reasonable policy. But we might well ask whether the critical state of affairs which now exists in Upper Clyde Shipbuilders would not have been recognized and the necessary corrective measures taken much earlier had we had a government of our own in Scotland.

In the last analysis, the question of the economic aspects of independence is a question of confidence. Do we have that confidence in our own ability which has been demonstrated by so many Scots people in so many parts of the world outside Scotland? If we have this confidence in exercising these abilities within Scotland, then the future should hold nothing for us but prosperity. But it is entirely up to us and if we choose independence, we choose to be judged by our own efforts and by nothing else. Correspondingly, we shall have no one but ourselves to blame should we fail. I believe that we shall not fail; indeed, I believe that political independence will bring Scotland more lasting prosperity than she has ever known before.

F

10

The Economic Case
against Independence

K. J. W. ALEXANDER

An economist invited to contribute an essay under the above title
has first to decide whether to examine in detail the policies of the
Scottish National Party or whether to examine the implications in
a more general way. The first approach has the attractions of
topicality and particularity, but would inevitably be desultory and
disconnected. The second approach would allow problems to be
examined in a more fundamental way, free from the taint of
political polemics. The more general approach has the additional
attraction that it must also have a bearing upon the argument
about more or less devolution, an issue which appears to have
more immediate and long-term importance than that of independence. In addition, any assessment of a particular set of policies
will have to be made with the help of a general analysis. For these
reasons this short essay will place its emphasis upon economic
principles. Reference to policy will be made by way of illustration,
but no full critique of S.N.P. policy is offered or claimed.

Although Scotland is better served with statistics than any of
the regions of Great Britain there are serious gaps which inhibit
the building of a macro-economic model of the economy of an
independent Scotland. Some of these statistical gaps exist because
within a Union, with free trade and a common fiscal system, the
case for distinguishing certain statistics on a regional basis is not
strong. For example, the Catto Report rejected 'a Border control
established for statistical purposes'.[1] The greater importance now
attached to regional policies strengthens the case for providing

[1] *Report of the Committee on Scottish Financial & Trade Statistics* (Cmnd.
8609, 1952, p. 75).

additional statistics, as does the apparent danger that when the full facts are not known the worst may be believed or feared. Some gaps in the official statistics have been filled by individual and institutional effort. Dr. Gavin McCrone has made notable scholarly contributions which will be drawn upon in what follows.[1] The Scottish Council (Development and Industry) has published statistics of Scottish exports.[2] There are no statistics, official, private, or even notional, of Scottish imports,[3] capital flows in and out, total savings, or total investment.

If a Scottish Government were to come into existence and it sought to manage an independent Scottish economy, much would depend upon the magnitude of some of these key determinants. Whereas a Scottish Government would be in a position—by economic management—to influence and alter some of these determinants, great importance would attach to the magnitude of these economic variables at the time of withdrawal from the U.K. Expressing the point in rather abstract Keynesian form, the relationship which is important can be expressed as:

$$S + T + M = I + G + X \tag{1}$$

with
$S = $ Savings $I = $ Investment
$T = $ Taxation $G = $ Government spending
$M = $ Imports $X = $ Exports

The items on the left-hand side of the equation may be thought of as those influences which drain purchasing power out of an economy and those on the right-hand side as influences which inject purchasing power into an economy. The equality between the two sides of this equation is an *ex post* equality, that is it is brought about by changes in the level of economic activity and national output. The two sides may equate at lower or higher levels. The problem of transition from a Union to two separate national economies is that, whereas for the Union the equality must hold, it is most unlikely that it will hold for its two parts which become

[1] Gavin McCrone, *Scotland's Economic Progress 1951–1960*, London, 1963 and *Scotland's Future: The Economics of Nationalism* (Oxford, 1969).

[2] *Exports Survey* (Scottish Council 1966) and *Visible Exports from Scotland to Countries outside the U.K. 1965–1967* (Scottish Council, 1969).

[3] Broad estimates of the foreign imports of Scotland for 1964 coming through all U.K. ports can be found in *Britain's Foreign Trade* (Port of London Authority), pages 66–7.

nations as a result of the process of disunion. This can be made more clear if we adapt equation (1) using the subscript u to indicate the Union, s for Scotland, and r for the rest of the Union (or rump).

$$S_u = S_s + S_r$$
$$T_u = T_s + T_r$$
$$I_u = I_s + I_r$$
$$G_u = G_s + G_r$$

The position of exports and imports is more complicated, as what is defined as external trade is necessarily increased by the act of disunion. The two-way flow of trade between Scotland and the rest of the United Kingdom which could be treated as internal specialization and division of labour within the Union must now be added to the foreign overseas trade of the two countries. Taking 'overseas' trade alone, and distinguishing it by the use of subscript o, the situation under the Union would be:

$$X_{uo} = X_{so} + X_{ro} \quad ; \quad M_{uo} = M_{so} + M_{ro}$$

The post-disunion situation can be illustrated as:
$$X_s = X_{so} + X_{sr}$$
$$M_s = M_{so} + M_{sr}$$
$$X_r = X_{ro} + X_{rs}$$
$$M_r = M_{ro} + M_{rs}$$

with
$$X_{rs} \equiv M_{sr}$$
and
$$X_{sr} \equiv M_{rs}$$

The situation under Union may now be expressed:

$$S_s + S_r + T_s + T_r + M_{so} + M_{ro} + [M_{sr} + M_{rs}]$$
$$= I_s + I_r + G_s + G_r + X_{ro} + X_{so} + [X_{sr} + X_{rs}] \qquad (2)$$

After disunion the immediate situation would be one of disequilibrium in both countries. Now while it is true that at any moment of time (as distinct from *ex post*) there will probably be an imbalance between the two sides of this equation in all national economies, there will have been forces—both market and governmental—working to minimize the extent of this disequilibrium.

Such forces will not have been at work to produce near-equilibrium within different regions of a national economy, however. Indeed, where central governments are committed to policies to reduce regional imbalance in incomes, etc., there is a likelihood that their policies of economic management will create and sustain inequalities between the two sides of the equation at the regional level. Even without such conscious acts of policy, however, it is most unlikely that the equation would hold to anything like the same extent at regional level as it does at national, so that after disunion the situation may be expressed as follows:

$$S_s + T_s + M_{so} + M_{sr} \gtrless I_s + G_s + X_{so} + X_{sr} \qquad (3)$$

and $$S_r + T_r + M_{ro} + M_{rs} \gtrless I_r + G_r + X_{ro} + X_{rs} \qquad (4)$$

If, when a Scottish Government took over, the left-hand side of the equation (3) were larger than the right-hand side there would be a tendency within Scotland to economic contraction. Indeed, the tendency would have existed prior to independence, but the post-independence statistics would reveal the cause. If there were unused resources in the Scottish economy this situation would be most favourable for a post-independence government. One of the most attractive of nationalist arguments rests on the assumption that this is in fact the situation. The argument is that because labour and some other factors of production are less fully employed in Scotland than in the rest of the U.K., the government of an independent Scotland would be able to apply expansionist policies of economic management without the same risk of 'over-heating' which inhibits British Governments from persevering with expansionist policies. This argument is made to appear even stronger when it is associated with the assertion that Scotland's balance of payments is sound and positive and would not impose the constraints upon rapid growth which have been associated with the overall U.K. balance of payments position.[1]

[1] For example, the speech made by Mr. Michael Grieve at his adoption as S.N.P. Parliamentary candidate for Govan: 'With independence we will also break away from the whole economic shambles which at present dictates the way we live in Scotland. . . . This economic problem, however, has nothing to do with Scotland. We have no balance of payments problem, no overconsumption.' (Quotation from *Scots Independent*, 1 February, 1969, of which paper Mr. Grieve is the editor.)

Whether such an expansionist policy would be open to an independent Scottish Government depends upon

(a) the extent of the unused resources in the Scottish economy;
(b) whether the left-hand side of equation (3) is larger than the right-hand; and
(c) whether, within the equation, Scotland does enjoy a balance of payments surplus of which the major trade component would be represented by $M_{so} + M_{sr} < X_{so} + X_{sr}$[1]

As has already been indicated, the statistics which could enable us to estimate all of these magnitudes do not exist, so that a complete analysis cannot be made. If trade flows are taken first there is no evidence for saying that Scotland would have a balance of trade surplus. The Scottish Council study suggests that the Scottish share of U.K. exports is 9·2 per cent, a creditable performance when her share of U.K. manufacturing output is 8·5 per cent. But these figures make no allowance for trade flows between Scotland and the rest of the U.K. Even within the Union there is need to take account of what proportion of Scottish overseas exports are based upon previous importation into Scotland—as, for example, of raw materials from abroad and components from south of the Border—and on this there are no statistics available. For this and other reasons it must be accepted that Scotland's present balance of trade is an unknown factor and that so is her balance of payments. When nationalist spokesmen have confidently expressed the view that Scotland has a balance of payments surplus they have probably been influenced by the Scottish Council study's suggestion that Scottish exports were a relatively high proportion of U.K. exports. But for a balance of trade figure an estimate of the relative or absolute amount of X_{so} is not enough. One could need estimates of X_{sr}, M_{so}, and M_{sr}, none of which is available.

What can be said, however, is that if the assertion that Scotland has a balance of trade surplus is adopted and in addition it is being assumed that the left-hand side of equation (3) is larger than the right-hand side, then because $M_{so} + M_{sr}$ is assumed to be less than $X_{so} + X_{sr}$, the imbalance which makes the left-hand side including imports larger than the right-hand side including exports must be

[1] For completeness the influence of tourism and of trade in invisibles should also be covered.

further accentuated when imports and exports are removed from the equation, leaving:

$$S_s + T_s > I_s + G_s.$$

This requirement would fit with another nationalist assumption, that the magnitude of taxes raised in Scotland is greater than the magnitude of government expenditures in Scotland. In this connection there is a complication which requires clarification. Some part of the administrative and other services 'bought' by taxes levied in Scotland are, within the Union, supplied from outside Scotland. Of these outside expenditures some would remain outside after independence—for example, expenditure on Embassies and representatives of Scotland's interests abroad (which would then be expanded to include the costs of representation in London) —whereas others would be brought within Scotland (for example, the expenditure on the administration provided from Whitehall ministries which would, after independence, take place in Scotland). These expenditures which moved into Scotland would make the size of G_s after disunion larger than before it. The most reliable estimate of the present situation is given by Dr. McCrone.[1] This suggests that the position in 1967 was as follows:

Total Revenue raised in Scotland (T_s)		£1,132m
Government expenditure (current) in Scotland, excluding defence	£792m	
Government expenditure (capital) in Scotland, excluding defence	£155m	
Government expenditure in Scotland on defence[2]	£160m	
Government payments of debt interest[3]	£105m	
Total government spending in Scotland (G_s)		£1,212m
Fiscal boost to Scottish economy		£80m

[1] *Scotland's Future*, pp. 57–8.

[2] Calculated as 6¾ per cent of U.K. total of £2388m. An S.N.P. research assistant has claimed that 'Scotland received some £90m less than her population share of defence expenditure in 1966–7' (*Glasgow Herald*, 14 March, 1969). My figures for 1967 would show Scotland receiving some £60m less than her share. The additional £30m claimed by the S.N.P. would not alter the overall picture.

[3] Dr. McCrone calculates this as Scotland's contributory share of a total U.K. debt interest transfer payment of £1,112, allocating Scotland's contribution on the basis of population at 9·4 per cent. I have made the additional assumption that the regional distribution of the U.K. national debt results in Scottish residents receiving a total debt interest also in proportion to population.

Moving from this to a post-independence situation would, as we have seen, require that additional expenditure currently taking place in Whitehall and Westminster were 'brought back' and made in Scotland. For 1967 the total of all outside expenditure was estimated as follows:

Defence[1]	£64m
External relations	£31m
Other	£36m
Total	£131m

At this point we must move from Dr. McCrone's careful estimate plus assumptions which have a fairly sound basis on to ground which is much less firm. What administrative costs additional to those already spent in Scotland would be increased within Scotland if there were an entirely separate legislature and executive in control of all internal and external policy? One may argue either that wasteful Whitehall methods would be avoided and Scotland could economize, or one could argue that the diseconomies of scale, the problems of independence, and the need to evolve cumbrous machinery for harmonizing Scottish policies with those of the rest of the U.K. would make independent government more expensive than Union government. My expectations lean to the second view, but to minimize dispute over a statistic which cannot be other than a rough estimate, I lean to the first view in my choice of a figure, and have taken £20m as the amount of government expenditure currently undertaken outside Scotland which independence would require to be made within Scotland leaving £111m as Scotland's expenditure on external relations, defence, etc. Adding this £20m to the previous figure of £1,212m for pre-independence spending we get post-independence expenditure of £1,232 (G_s), so that the fiscal boost to the economy, $T_s - G_s$, would be:

Expenditure	£1,232m
Taxation	£1,132m
	£100m[2]

[1] £224m, as Scotland's population share, less £16om spent in Scotland.

[2] Throughout I have used one of the three alternative assumptions made by Dr. McCrone that Scotland's share of unallocated expenditure be calculated at 9·4 per cent, based on population. This seems the most reasonable if one is concerned with the provision of services. If the assumption at the other extreme is made, the above estimate of fiscal boost would fall to approximately £77m.

It should be noted that the residual £111m (£131m outside expenditure, minus £20m 'brought back') would worsen the Scottish balance of payments position, either by reducing any surplus or increasing any deficit by that amount.

It is probably desirable to recapitulate at this stage of the argument. Taking equation (3) as a macro-economic model for a post-independence Scotland, we expressed the nationalist belief that a Scottish government could adopt an expansionist policy as being a situation in which the magnitude of the left-hand side of the relationship was greater than that of the right-hand side. In the absence of any reliable statistics for Scotland's balance of trade, we pointed out that for the nationalist assumptions about the scope of expansion to be compatible with the assertion that Scotland does and would enjoy a balance of payments surplus, requires that

$$S_s + T_s > I_s + G_s$$

Having now explored the relationship between T_s and G_s the conclusion is that T_s was less than G_s by around £100m in 1967. Thus we are left with the relationship between S_s and I_s, and for this to make the nationalist expansionist assumptions and balance of trade assertions compatible would require that

$$S_s > I_s + £100m.$$

Here again we are frustrated by the absence of complete statistics. Scotland's higher *per capita* involvement in National Savings has led some to assume that Scotland saves more per head than the rest of the U.K. There is no firm evidence for this, however, and some pointers to the opposite conclusion. Firstly, the distribution of personal assets held by Scots indicates a stronger preference for the 'official savings media' north of the Border than south of it. In addition Scottish-held personal assets as a percentage of all holdings in Great Britain in 1965 at 7·2 per cent (of gross wealth) and 7·4 per cent (of net wealth) do not suggest that savings in Scotland have been higher than in the rest of Britain.[1] Lastly the lower levels of Scottish incomes would lead one to expect that even if the proportion of incomes saved were

[1] L. C. Wright, 'Personal Wealth in Scotland and Great Britain', *The Three Banks Review* (No. 179, September, 1968).

F*

higher than in the rest of the U.K., the absolute amount of savings per head would be lower. In fact, it appears that Scottish *per capita* expenditure is closer to the British average (93 per cent) than is Scottish income (which is around 10 per cent below the U.K. average). It would thus seem that to allocate Scotland a *per capita* share of all U.K. saving would be to exaggerate considerably the volume of Scottish thrift. Such a *per capita* share could be £540m, which is used more to avoid unnecessary dispute than out of any conviction.

On the investment side, again there is no one comprehensive statistic. A figure of £575m seems a reasonable estimate for investment in Scotland net of government investment,[1] so that the relationship required to sustain nationalist assumptions and assertions

$$S_s > I_s + £100\text{m}$$

does not hold with

$$S_s = £540\text{m and } I_s = £575\text{m.}$$

It should be remembered that the value given to S_s is probably over-generous. My conclusion so far is that the nationalist expectation that with independence it would be possible to launch an expansionist policy of economic management would be frustrated because the assumptions on which it rests are incompatible, given the magnitude of *some* of the components of the model. It is not possible to assert with complete confidence that the expectations would also be frustrated as a result of the sum total of the magnitudes involved on both sides of the model, as statistics are not available for some of the components.

If it is accepted that T_s is less than G_s and that S_s is less than I_s, the balancing factor for a Scottish economy would have to be M_s is greater than X_s, at least for the short term during which internal adjustments could be made. It is this imbalance which leads me to the view that with independence Scotland would either have to expand production to enable us to enjoy our pre-independence standard of living or to cut back consumption, investment,

---

[1] Statistics for U.K. investment have been scaled down using the 8.5 per cent figure for the proportion which Scotland's G.D.P. forms of U.K. G.D.P. Statistics from the *Digest of Scottish Statistics* have been used where available, making deductions for investment grants.

or government expenditure very considerably. There is considerable economic slack to be taken up in Scotland, but I doubt whether it comes near in magnitude to the imbalance which would have to be bridged if independence were not to result in a fall in the standard of living. If one assumes a reduction of unemployment to 30,000 and an increase in the activity rate to the present U.K. average, a rough calculation suggests that the increase in Scottish national product could be of the order of £80m. If this could be achieved it would certainly cause 'over-heating' within Scotland. The consequent inflationary pressures would make the achievement of a balance of payments surplus more difficult than before. The difficulty could be abolished—along with all other economic problems—by assuming that independence will so change attitudes and increase efficiency that there will be a very rapid growth in Scottish production as a direct consequence of independence.[1] This is the equivalent of the naïve Socialist belief that nationalization will by itself lead to increased economic efficiency, and would provide an equally insecure basis on which to make policy decisions.

Dr. Simpson appears to recognize, at least implicitly, the need for Scotland to correct an unfavourable balance of payments when he writes: 'It would probably be wise to adopt a floating exchange rate. It is simply nonsense to say Scotland could not devalue successfully.'[2] Such a devaluation, if successful, would be no more than one way of adapting to the lower standard of living resulting from independence. Even if coupled with a successful policy of expansion which overcame counteracting inflationary pressures, the magnitude of unemployed resources available to be brought into activity would only offset a proportion (I suggest under half) of the cut in the standard of living resulting from the ending of the inter-regional redistribution of income within the U.K. which currently operates in Scotland's favour.

In conclusion, it is probably as well to make clear that the fact that independence would worsen rather than better Scotland's economic situation is not, in my view, an overwhelming argument against either complete independence or an increase in self-

---

[1] Dr. Simpson makes this assumption (p. 128) and I comment upon it (p. 144) later in this volume.

[2] David Simpson, 'Puerile Probe (on facts of life) by Dr. McCrone', *Scots Independent*, 24 May, 1969.

government. I do regard it as an overwhelming argument against the S.N.P., however. As part of its campaign to induce people to support it as the political vehicle for the achievement of independence, the S.N.P. uses arguments which are the antithesis of economic reality: 'This huge subsidy to England (over £3 per week for each Scottish household) could be used by a Scottish government to tackle so many of the problems pressing on Scotland at this moment.'[1] Whereas all political parties put their own gloss on economic facts and analysis, the S.N.P. has built its political programme around a central economic fallacy which rests on a multitude of economic fictions.[2] It is the economics of the S.N.P. more than the economics of the country itself which convinces me that independence would be a desolating experience for Scotland:

Want o' wit is waur than want o' gear.

[1] *Clearway Ahead for Scotland*, S.N.P., n.d.

[2] The fictions change. On the budgetary position it has been interesting to watch the different versions in the main policy document *S.N.P. and You*. In 1964 the claim was 'This whip-hand discretion against Scotland amounted, in direct taxation alone, to at least another £1,000m in the last 10 years. This is the amount, based on government figures and conservative estimates, which you have paid to London and which was neither spent in Scotland, nor for the benefit of Scotland.' In 1966 the figure was £1,250m, and by 1968 it was £1,250m 'since 1952'. Thus we have:

1954–63—£1,000m over 10 years, averaging £100m p.a.
1956–65—£1,250m over 10 years, averaging £125m p.a.

which would imply a rapidly worsening rate of exploitation of Scotland by London.

1952–67—£1,250m over 16 years, averaging £78m p.a.,

which when taken with the two earlier claims would imply either that 1952–3 were years in which the 'whip-hand' had been exercised massively in Scotland's favour or that in 1966–7 the earlier tendency to 'exploitation' had been dramatically reversed. My own conclusion is that it is unreasonable to expect economic fiction to pass a consistency test.

11 *a*

A Reply to Dr. Simpson

K. J. W. ALEXANDER

In my essay I have concentrated on the macro-economics of independence, reaching conclusions which harden me in my opinion that independence would add to the difficulties of getting economic activity in Scotland on to a firmer basis from which self-sustained growth will be possible. Dr. Simpson holds the opposite opinion. His essay has little to say on the macro-economics of independence, but concentrates on a number of economic arguments which have been advanced against independence.[1] It is hoped that a few comments by Dr. Simpson and myself on each other's essays will help the reader to form an opinion of his own.

It is necessary to distinguish between the 'psychology of dependence' arguments which Dr. Simpson deploys and the 'economics of independence' issue. Psychology does seem to be at the heart of the matter. When Dr. Simpson expresses his concern at the idea of 'the Westminster Government being a charitable dispenser of unearned benefits', and garnishes his argument with references to begging-bowls, vending-machines, and pork-barrels, this does not reflect any *laissez faire* view of what governments should or should not do. I do not doubt that in an independent Scotland Dr. Simpson would favour government action to re-allocate income on a regional basis. He might even spare the Highlanders and the Borderers the charge of brandishing their begging-bowls for charity from an Edinburgh government. The root of his argument

---

[1] Readers who wish to study these arguments in their original form will find them in an article by the present author in *Scotland*, vol. 12, No. 5, May, 1968; and, with more detail and sophistication, in G. McCrone, *Scotland's Future* (Oxford, 1969) especially Chapter IV.

is psychological not economic, and is that the Westminster Government cannot be his government. The point comes out clearly again in his argument that 'tak[ing] the responsibility for running our own affairs' will, through 'learning by doing' produce greater efficiency. The issue is not one of democracy and participation alone. Switzerland is held up as a model, yet in that country Mrs. Ewing would not have the opportunity of 'learning by doing' which she now has. Dr. Simpson's approach is probably affected, as my own is, by the belief that democratic participation can be more effective in smaller-scale organizations. Scotland, with its distinctive history, culture, law, etc., is an attractive smaller base on which to put this belief to the test. However, even if the context of our debate were not explicitly economic I would urge on Dr. Simpson that it is more sensible to relate decisions about the optimum scale of operations to the functions to be performed than to a 'sense of national identity' as interpreted by a person or group of persons. Once effective and functional machinery has been decided upon it should be established so that there is the maximum democratic participation and control over the decision-taking of the executives responsible for each function or group of functions. Dr. Simpson's approach seems strongly coloured by the view that his 'own affairs' stop at the Border. My approach is coloured by the view that there are functions affecting people who live to the north and the south of that Border which are better performed by an executive and controlled by a legislature elected by all those affected on either side of it.

A related issue arises when Dr. Simpson argues that 'there is considerable evidence to suggest that our efforts [that is the efforts of the working members of the Scottish community] will be increased following independence, since people will feel that they have something worth working for.' None of the evidence is cited and I find it difficult to accept that what we have here is anything more than a reflection of Dr. Simpson's own views and his faith that these are widely shared. After all, we do know that, even at its 1968 peak of popularity, the S.N.P. received only a minority vote in the majority of elections and that only a proportion of those who vote for it want independence. Thus if only a minority want independence, how can Dr. Simpson claim that increased efforts at work would result from it? If he can argue that those who oppose the Union would work harder if it were broken up, is it not equally possible that the many more who favour the Union would work less hard after independence?[1]

In all of these arguments I suggest that Dr. Simpson is projecting his own feelings of alienation from the Union, Westminster government, etc., assuming that these feelings are widely shared and that they thus provide a firm basis on which to build economic arguments. It is not Dr. Simpson's economics that are 'separatist' but his psychology.

On the fiscal issue Dr. Simpson gives as his opinion, which he claims is not contradicted by the available evidence, 'that we in Scotland have contributed at least as much to the Westminster Government in the form of taxes and other government revenues as we have ever received from it in the form of government expenditures'. It would be of great interest to have his views of Dr. McCrone's estimates which I have used in my essay.

I have argued that the high degree of inter-dependence between the Scottish part of the U.K. economy and the rest of that economy would greatly limit the extent to which an independent Scottish government could carry out a genuinely independent economic policy.[2] This inter-dependence arises not only because of the very strong trade ties between the two parts of the U.K. economy, but also because of the long-established high mobility of capital and labour in both directions. Independence would involve creating two economies out of what has been for more than two centuries a unified market for products, labour, and capital. Dr. Simpson suggests that, if this argument were true, unionists would have nothing to worry about, as independence would change nothing. This overlooks the fiscal consequences of disunion and ignores the importance of having some direct influence on economic decision-taking within what must always remain the largest part of the economy of the British Isles. On this Dr. Simpson says 'it is difficult to see what the results of this influence have been'. Within an economy the size of the U.K. many developments are only possible given a firm understanding that these complement

[1] Note, for example, the view endorsed unanimously at the 72nd Annual Congress of the Scottish Trades Unions in April 1969: '. . . complete political and economic sovereignty would represent a retrograde step which would set back substantially the hopes and expectations of the Scottish people'. Is it likely that, believing this, Scottish trades unionists would feel that after disunion they had 'something worth working for'?

[2] *Scotland*, op. cit.

rather than compete with other developments planned and under consideration. Without machinery to rationalize investment decisions in this way there would be considerable risk of competitive over-investment, probably backed by public subsidy. Within the machinery for taking such decisions Scotland has done remarkably well, with the reactor in Caithness, the aluminium smelter on the Moray Firth, the container berth on the Clyde, the Institution of Advanced Machine Tool Technology at East Kilbride, and the Centre for Industrial Innovation at Strathclyde. The decisions which led to the expansion of the Scottish vehicle industry at Bathgate and at Linwood were also of this type.

I suggest that without 'U.K.-wide' decision-taking several of these developments could not have been embarked upon with any confidence by an independent Scottish government. These developments exist to serve a market of which the rest of the U.K. makes up a substantial part. If those deciding to serve that market from Scotland had felt that those making decisions south of the Border had no interest in the success of investment north of it (because they had no part in the decision which led to its being made), I suggest that in a number of cases at least the decision to go ahead in Scotland would not have been taken. Machinery for harmonization could, of course, be worked out, but this would be more cumbersome, time-wasting, and expensive than the machinery which operates at present, and it would be a recognition that 'independence' was a slogan rather than an economic practicality.

Dr. Simpson caps his view that such inter-dependence is not a serious problem with the somewhat contradictory suggestion that an independent Scottish government would 'try to lessen her dependence on the markets of only one country'. In dealing with the negotiations on the future of trade between Scotland and the rest of the U.K. which would be necessary after independence he argues that because 'Scotland forms by no means a negligible market for English goods', therefore 'England has a very similar interest in maintaining free and stable trading relationships with Scotland'. I cannot accept this argument. Suppose, for the purposes of illustration only, that 2 per cent of the value of the manufacturing output of the rest of the U.K. is exported to Scotland. Making the further assumption that there is a balance of trade in manufactures between the two states, this would mean that Scotland would be exporting 22 per cent of the value of her manufacturing output to the rest of the U.K. This is no more than a specific example of the obvious fact that small nations are usually much more dependent on trade than are larger nations.

The Republic of Ireland is cited as an example of how an independent economic policy may be pursued even when there is a high degree of trade dependence. The very much lower average income in Eire is noted as additional proof that Scotland could 'do it'. In fact it is this much lower standard of living which has given the government of Eire a little elbow room within which to exercise a very limited degree of real independence in economic affairs, and in particular to attract new industry. If the wages gap between Irish and U.K. workers were narrowed to that which exists between the average for workers in Scotland and workers in the rest of the U.K., the room for manoeuvre by the Irish Government would be much reduced.[1] Neither this argument, nor the persistence of Eire's very much lower standard of living on which it is based, should commend themselves to Scots on economic grounds.

On the key issue of regional policy within a Union versus an independent economic policy for growth, I have argued that the macro-economic situation faced by a Scottish government upon the break-up of the Union would frustrate the adoption of any effective growth policy. I have argued elsewhere that independence would cost Scotland the benefits of the present policy of diverting industry from the more to the less prosperous parts of the U.K.[2] Dr. Simpson claims that this argument suffers from 'three basic flaws'. Firstly, because Scotland is only one of several development regions, Dr. Simpson argues that the Board of Trade has no particular reason to favour Scotland. The logic of the situation is surely that if the Board of Trade favours development areas at the expense of non-development areas and if, as a result, Scotland gets any expansion which would not otherwise have come there, this is a gain which would be lost as a consequence of independence. The second 'flaw' is that 'there is very little evidence that . . . the issuing of Industrial Development Certificates has

---

[1] An estimate for 1963 put the earnings of male industrial workers in Eire at 70 per cent of the U.K. level (P. R. Kaim-Caudle, *Social Security in Ireland and Western Europe*, The Economic Research Institute, Dublin, 1964).

[2] *Scotland*, op. cit.

had much influence in causing firms to relocate'. The most comprehensive evidence available suggests that between 1956 and 1967 estimated additional employment of 166,000 came to Scotland as a result of this policy.[1] 'In 1968 there was a threefold increase in industrial development certificate approvals in development areas compared with the average of 1961–1963. In the rest of the country, the increase was less than a third. This indicates that the total development area package is now having a very marked effect.'[2]

It can be argued that Scotland has not had her 'share' of jobs originating in all other areas. From 1966 to 1968 Scotland received 29 per cent of these moves, although Scottish employment makes up 44 per cent of all employment in development areas. This shortfall is more a function of distance, geography, and structural economic factors which would not be abolished by an act of disunion. Table 2 in the Board of Trade study, *The Movement of Manufacturing Industry in the U.K.* 1945–65 (H.M.S.O., 1968), makes it clear that a major aspect of the Scottish problem has been the internal rate of decline in jobs in the manufacturing sector. Over the period 1953 to 1966 there were only three regions which suffered an internal net decline, Northern Ireland losing 25,000 jobs, Scotland losing 51,000, and the north-western region losing 109,000. The situation in Scotland has been considerably eased by the inward movement of 50,000 jobs by 1965, leaving an approximate change in manufacturing employment of 1,000 jobs. Only the north-western region enjoyed a larger inward movement, of 68,000 jobs; but in relation to both the total employment in the region and to the internal net loss of jobs, the inflow was markedly favourable to Scotland. The changes in unemployment in the development areas between June 1963 and April 1969 also indicate that Scottish problems have been tackled with relative success. The regions with increased numbers unemployed were: south-western, with an increase of 2,793, northern with 6,692, and Wales with 7,006. Regions with decreased unemployment were Merseyside with a decrease of 8,684 and Scotland with a decrease of 15,764.

Dr. Simpson's third argument is that independence would free

---

[1] *The Intermediate Areas*, Cmnd. 3998, H.M.S.O., 1969, App. 6. The Board of Trade recognizes that there is some exaggeration by applicants for industrial development certificates in development areas and that this statistic will probably be an over-estimate.

[2] *The Intermediate Areas*, p. 143.

Scotland to offer more discriminating inducements. I have advocated more such flexibility and discrimination over many years, but never at the expense of a comprehensive and compatible policy of industrial relocation within the U.K. economy. Dr. Simpson underestimates the capacity of pressure-groups in, for example, north-east England and Merseyside to insist that the regional inducements they could offer would always compete effectively with whatever inducements were offered by an independent Scottish government.

A personal involvement prevents me from commenting in detail on Dr. Simpson's version of the difficulties of shipbuilding on Upper Clyde. It is, however, within my personal knowledge that the Secretary of State and the Scottish Office were involved throughout the crisis, and in my opinion this involvement contributed to a more satisfactory outcome than looked possible in its early stages.

11b

A Reply to Professor Alexander

DAVID SIMPSON

Professor Alexander's paper is largely devoted to one issue, the question of whether or not there will be a balance of payments deficit following independence. Professor Alexander tries to show that there will be, and that a fall in the standard of living is inevitable. I have never denied the possibility of a balance of payments deficit after independence (see my paper, page 127). What I do deny is the inevitability of a fall in the standard of living.

The standard of living in the long run, say from five years after Independence, does not depend of course upon subsidies of government but upon the efforts of the people. The relationship between the longer- and the shorter-run standard of living is this: if the long-run standard of living is rising, then there exists a variety of adjustment mechanisms such that a deficit in the short-run balance of payments can be financed without a fall in the short-run standard of living. I have considered these various adjustment mechanisms elsewhere (*Scottish Independence: An Economic Analysis*).[1] The recent history of the U.K. balance of payments provides ample illustration of how a substantial deficit in the balance of payments may be financed without a fall in the standard of living. There are many countries throughout the world whose positions in one degree or another are comparable to those of Scotland. These countries have invariably experienced rising standards of living in the post-war period. I do not know of the existence of any special factors which would prevent Scotland emulating the performance of those countries in raising their standard of living. And so I find it difficult to accept the idea that

[1] Edinburgh, 1969.

150

the standard of living in Scotland will not rise in the long run. To the best of my knowledge unionist commentators have never advanced any reasons to show that the standard of living in Scotland will decline in the long run. If it did, it would certainly be exceptional, since the number of countries in the world whose standard of living is declining is extremely small, and those that are in this category are in circumstances wholly outside the experience of Scotland.

I have always been sceptical of the connection between the purely economic aspects of independence and the political issues. The substance of Professor Alexander's article is simply that the existence of a balance of payments deficit following independence constitutes an argument against political independence. His article is, indeed, entitled 'The Economic Case Against Independence', yet this is a very strange argument. The United Kingdom has been a net borrower of short-term capital on a considerable scale from Switzerland, as well as from the International Monetary Fund. Yet no one seriously suggests that this constitutes an argument for the United Kingdom becoming a *canton* of Switzerland. Attempts to estimate Government revenue and expenditure in Scotland have always seemed to me to be unrewarding exercises,[1] for several reasons: the unreliability of the available information, the confusion between public expenditure in Scotland and what is spent by government agencies located in Scotland, the confusion between public expenditure in Scotland and the benefits which accrue to the people of Scotland from public expenditure and, above all, the irrelevance of public expenditure today to public expenditure after Independence.

While I am quite willing, purely for the sake of the present argument, to accept Professor Alexander's claim of the existence of an £80m surplus of public expenditure over revenue in 1967,[2] I cannot accept his suggestion that G_s would necessarily rise after independence (see page 137). The reduction of defence expenditure to a level of £100m would alone affect a saving of £60m on

[1] This view would appear to be shared by the Chancellor of the Exchequer (see *The Scotsman*, 27 June, 1969). The major item of interest, the public sector balance, is obtained as the difference between two much larger figures, both of which are subject to errors.

[2] In order to put this figure in perspective it is worth recalling that the *additional* taxation raised in Scotland by the budgets of 1968 would be about £100m.

Professor Alexander's figures.[1] On pages 138–42 of his paper Professor Alexander tries to make the transition from an £80m deficit on the public sector account in 1967 to an unspecified deficit on the balance of payments account in the future. The issues seem confused rather than clarified by his methodology. He appears (page 141) to assert that the elimination of the deficit will inevitably lead to a fall in the standard of living. While acknowledging the possibility of 'taking up slack', he appears to overlook the possibility of other methods of adjustment such as foreign borrowing and re-allocation of government expenditure. So long as long-run real output per head is rising, I do not see why these and other measures should not be able to bridge the deficit in the balance of payments without causing a fall in the standard of living.

In this connection, Professor Alexander (page 141) misplaces my point about the standard of living. Naturally, I do not suppose that any balance of payments deficit will be overcome by an overnight transformation of popular efforts and skills. My point was that the long-run standard of living of Scotland, as of every other country, is dependent upon these real factors and not upon subsidies, actual or alleged. I know of no reason why our efforts, skill, and judgment should diminish in the future. Professor Alexander's surprising remark that the 'S.N.P. has built its political programme around a central economic fallacy which rests on a multitude of economic fictions' must be judged against his opening statement that 'no full critique of S.N.P. policy is offered or claimed', which is borne out by the text. There is nothing in his footnote on page 142 to suggest that the annual revisions in *S.N.P. and You* are any more 'fictional' than the annual revisions in the Blue Book *National Income and Expenditure*. Whatever the faults of the S.N.P., and it has its share, its official spokesmen do not knowingly try to mislead the people of Scotland.[2]

---

[1] In his first paragraph Professor Alexander says he doesn't wish to consider S.N.P. policy, but this seems a little academic in the context of his concluding paragraph.

[2] Referring to the preliminary results of a Treasury investigation, Mr. Roy Jenkins, Chancellor of the Exchequer, said: 'On the basis of these figures, Scotland would not be economically viable if separated from the rest of the U.K.' Since he was addressing the Council of the Scottish Chambers of Commerce this was naturally the lead story in *The Scotsman* under the headline 'Treasury Inquiry Shows Scotland Can't Pay Way, Says Chancellor' (*The Scotsman*

Finally, let me match Professor Alexander's concluding aphorism with one of my own. It seems to me that the dread with which so many unionists contemplate the responsibilities of self-government is aptly summarized in Hilaire Belloc's lines:

> And always keep a-hold of Nurse
> For fear of finding something worse.

---

27 June, 1969). Next day in an obscure paragraph on an inside page, Mr. Jenkins was quoted as saying 'This doesn't mean it couldn't if it chose to do so, pay its way; all it does mean is that I think the way would be rockier' (*The Scotsman*, 28 June, 1969).

INDEX

Adamson, William, M.P., 13.
Advocates, Faculty of, 40.
Afrikaans language, 25.
Agricultural Revolution, 7, 105, 110.
Angell, Norman, 115.
Anglophobia, 24–5, 119.
Argyll, 5.
Asquith, H. H., 11, 81.
Assimilation, Scotland with England, 36, 41, 48, 95.
Attlee, Clement, 16–18.
Austria, 27.
Austro-Hungarian Empire, 6, 28fn.
Australia, 7, 86, 110; federalism in, 86.
Aytoun, Professor W. E., 8.

Balance of payments, 127, 133–41, 150.
Balfour, A. J., 8, 11, 106.
Balfour of Burleigh, 8.
Balfour, 2nd Earl, 18–19.
Barr, Rev. James, M.P., 14–15, 20, 79.
Barron, Evan McLeod, 24.
Bavaria, 27, 114.
Belfast, 113.
Belhaven, Lord, 35.
Bell, Professor G. J., 40.
Biafra, 28.
Birkenhead, Earl of, 46.
Bismarck, 22, 23, 26, 111.
Board of Trade, 59, 97, 125, 147–8.
Boers, 22, 25.
Borders, The, 113, 143.
Boswell, James, 7.
Bovey, Keith, 115.
British way of life, 54, 103–11.
Brittany, 112.
Bruce, Robert, King of Scots, 26.
Buchan, Norman, M.P., 116–17.
Buchanan, George, M.P., 13.
Budget, Scottish, 71, 72, 97, 123.
Burns, Robert, 7, 26, 108.
Burns, Thomas, 17.

Caithness, 9, 113.
Campbell, Sir Graham, M.P., 8.
Campbell-Bannerman, Sir Henry, 10, 11.

Canada, 6, 7, 18, 57, 86, 109, 110; federalism in, 18, 57, 86.
Catto, Lord, 18, 132.
Cavour, 26, 111.
Cecil, Robert, 115.
Centralization, 53–5, 57, 82–3, 95–9, 116, 129.
Centre for Industrial Innovation, 146.
Chapple, Dr., M.P., 11.
China, 23, 31.
Church of Scotland, 7, 24, 54, 66, 88, 94–5, 105, 107, 111, 117.
Churchill, Sir Winston, 19.
Clark, Dr. G. B., M.P., 9.
Clyde, River, 106, 109, 110, 111, 113, 118, 130, 146.
Cockburn, Lord, 39, 48.
Codification of law, 41–2, 44, 47.
Committee on Scottish Financial and Trade Statistics ('Catto Committee'), 18, 132.
Common Market—see European Communities.
Commonwealth, 12, 14, 30, 61, 62.
Communist Party, 91.
Confederation, 58, 63, 86–8.
Confidence, 51, 60, 68, 131.
Conservative Party: and English Nationalism, 30; and Scottish Policy, 18–20, 30, 67, 74, 77, 91, 92, 100–1, 120, 122.
Constitution, written, 39, 47–8, 56–7, 80, 87.
Constitutional change: arguments against, 103–20; cultural consequences, 68, 77; economic consequences, 121–53; justification, need for, 103; legal consequences, 34–51; possible forms of, 52–5, 65–79, 80–8, 97–102; processes of, 52, 58–64.
Convention of Royal Burghs, 8, 14.
Cooper, Lord President, 35, 39, 41 fn, 42, 43, 47.
Cooperative Party, 13.
Coudenhove-Kalergi, Count, 115.
Court of Session, 38.
Cowan, Sir W. H., M.P., 11.
Cripps, Sir Stafford, 16.